THE ORIGINS
OF THE
CHRISTIAN DOCTRINE
OF
SACRIFICE

BY

ROBERT J. DALY, S.J.

FORTRESS PRESS
PHILADELPHIA

To Mother

Biblical quotations from the Revised Standard Version of the Bible, copyright 1946, 1952, © 1971, 1973 by the Division of Christian Education of the National Council of the Churches of Christ in the U.S.A., are used by permission.

Library of Congress Cataloging in Publication Data

Daly, Robert J.   1933-
    The origins of the Christian doctrine of sacrifice.

    Includes indexes.
    1. Sacrifice—Biblical teaching.   2. Sacrifice—History of doctrines.   I. Title.
BS680.S2D34   232'.4   77-78628
ISBN 0-8006-1267-1

6455G77   Printed in the United States of America   1-1267

CONTENTS

ABBREVIATIONS

CS	Robert J. Daly, *Christian Sacrifice: The Judaeo-Christian Background before Origen* (Studies in Christian Antiquity 18; Washington: The Catholic University of America Press, 1978)
AB	Anchor Bible
AnBib	Analecta biblica
ANF	The Ante-Nicene Fathers
Bib	*Biblica*
BZ	*Biblische Zeitschrift*
BZAW	Beihefte zur *Zeitschrift für die alttestamentliche Wissenschaft*
CBQ	*Catholic Biblical Quarterly*
GCS	Griechische christliche Scriftsteller
HNT	Handbuch zum Neuen Testament
HTKNT	Herders theologischer Kommentar zum Neuen Testament
HTR	*Harvard Theological Review*
MeyerK	H. A. W. Meyer, Kritischexegetischer Kommentar über das Neue Testament
NovTSup	Novum Testamentum, Supplements
NTabh	Neutestamentliche Abhandlungen
NTS	*New Testament Studies*
PG	J. Migne, *Patrologia graeca*
RB	*Revue biblique*
RNT	Regensburger Neues Testament
SANT	Studien zum Alten und Neuen Testament
SC	Sources chrétiennes
SNTSMS	Society for New Testament Studies Monograph Series
SPB	Studia postbiblica
TDNT	G. Kittel and G. Friedrich, eds., *Theological Dictionary of the New Testament*
TU	Texte und Untersuchungen
WMANT	Wissenschaftliche Monographien zum Alten und Neuen Testament
ZA	*Zeitschrift für Assyriologie*
ZNW	*Zeitschrift für die neutestamentliche Wissenschaft*

FOREWORD

Basic to an understanding of Christianity is the concept of Christian sacrifice. In most religions where it is found, the practice of sacrifice stands at the center of a dynamic process in which the divine and the human come into contact. This is particularly true of biblical Judaism. For, as it relived its various covenantal experiences in the course of celebrating its ongoing love affair with Yahweh, ancient Israel made use of an elaborate sacrificial ritual.

This alone would make an understanding of sacrifice of cardinal importance for the Christian. For, lying at the heart of the Christian message, going back to Christ himself, is the idea that this new covenant does not so much abolish the old as bring it to its divinely ordained fulfillment. Christians, therefore, cannot avoid asking themselves: What role does sacrifice have in my Christian belief and practice? It was central to Old Testament religion. Is it central to mine? If so, in what way? Christians posing these questions will also be at least generally aware that the New Testament uses sacrificial language and imagery to speak of the Christ-event, and that Paul in particular uses them to speak of Christian life itself. What does this language mean? Does it have a realistic meaning? Or is it intended only metaphorically? Whatever the answer, even widely differing interpreters recognize the need for understanding the background and context of the way the New Testament kerygma uses sacrificial language and imagery.

But these questions have merely scratched the surface. For sacrificial language and imagery are found not only in the New Testament kerygma; they are still alive among Christians today. Most Christians are familiar with the concept "the sacrifice of Christ," or with the idea of "offering up" the gift of good works or service. Many are also familiar with the concept of the Eucharist as sacrifice. In fact, during the twelve years in which

I have been researching this theme, I have been struck by the number of times in which people assumed that by "sacrifice" I meant "Eucharist." Although most of these people were in fact Roman Catholics, it has become increasingly clear that a close connection between Eucharist and sacrifice is not just a Roman Catholic perception. It has moved close to the center of ecumenical theological dialogue.[1] It was, for example, one of the central themes for discussion at the Ecumenical Theological Symposium on the Eucharist held on the occasion of the Forty-first International Eucharistic Congress at Philadelphia, August 3–5, 1976. This ecumenical situation allows us to hope that polemical polarizations are a thing of the past, and that we will be able to investigate such questions as this with minds and hearts more humbly open to the one Spirit of Truth.

In this mood of honest search we put the question: Are the language and imagery of sacrifice which we Christians still use merely an expendable residue, the metaphorical remains of a manner of worship now totally superseded? A simple "yes" or "no" cannot do justice to the complexity of this question. For ultimately we are talking about the Christ-event, and our lives are truly Christian only to the extent that we participate in the Christ-event. Since, therefore, the Christ-event is clearly presented to us in the New Testament as a sacrificial event, our participation in Christ is necessarily sacrificial in some truly significant way. However, Christian life itself is not primarily a ritual celebration, nor merely an intellectual adherence to a body of truths; it is primarily a participation in Christ by means of personal commitment to an active life of service and self-giving love. What, then, do we mean when we speak of this life as "sacrificial"? Our investigation into the origins of the Christian theology of sacrifice will, I hope, enable us to answer this question in a way that will be illuminating for all Christians.

1. Cf. *The Eucharist as Sacrifice,* published jointly by representatives of the U.S.A. National Committee of the Lutheran World Federation and the Bishop's Committee for Ecumenical and Interreligious Affairs (New York: U.S.A. National Committee for Lutheran World Federation/Washington: U.S. Catholic Conference, 1967) see esp. pp. 188–91. See also L. Swidler, ed., *The Eucharist in Ecumenical Perspective,* a special issue of the *Journal of Ecumenical Studies* 13:2 (Spring 1976).

Chapter One introduces the main body of the work with discussions of the meaning of the word "sacrifice," the general theory of sacrifice, and the concept of "spiritualization." Chapter Two treats the biblical foundations in the two main types of Old Testament sacrifice, the burnt offering and sacrifices of atonement. This chapter also discusses ancient Israel's awareness of the need for the divine acceptance of sacrifice. Chapter Three, after indicating the role played by the Septuagint Greek translation of the Scriptures in supplying the sacrificial language used by the Christians of New Testament times, gathers together those aspects of the history of sacrifice in late Old Testament and early rabbinic times which are most helpful in understanding the transition of sacrificial ideas from the Old to the New Testament. These are the covenant sacrifice, the Passover, the significance of the blood of circumcision, the Qumran (Dead Sea Scrolls) idea of the community itself as God's temple, and the Akedah (Jewish interpretation of the sacrifice of Isaac).

Chapter Four treats the New Testament understanding of sacrifice as found in the Synoptics, Acts, Paul, Hebrews, John, and the Book of Revelation. Here we uncover our two central findings. The first is that the three aspects of the Pauline theology of sacrifice—the sacrifice of Christ, Christians as the new temple, and the sacrifices of Christians—provide an outline for a true theology of sacrifice for the church. The second is that the idea of Christian sacrificial activity as found in Paul and the rest of the New Testament is not primarily ritualistic or liturgical, but above all ethical and practical. This chapter also includes a section on the temple as community in Qumran and the New Testament and another on the history-of-religions context of "worship in spirit and in truth."

Chapter Five, guided by the two main findings of the New Testament chapter, follows the development of the Christian idea of sacrifice in the early church, beginning with the Apostolic Fathers and moving through the apologists, Justin and Athenagoras, and up to Irenaeus and Hippolytus. Next, two second century Passover treatises and the second century Acts of the Martyrs are treated. Finally, the Alexandrian tradition, from Philo through Barnabas to Clement, is given attention. I round off this historical treatment at about the year 200 (but including Hippolytus), and finish it with a brief sketch of Origen's idea of Christian life as sacrifice. A fully adequate treatment of Origen would require more space than is available. Tertullian and Cyprian are absent for somewhat the same reason. They will be taken up in another work which will study the idea of sacrifice as it developed in the Latin tradition from Tertullian and the *Vetus Latina* up to Leo.

Chapter Five closes with a sketch of the Eucharist as sacrifice in the early church. Here, for the first time, I change my focus and try to look specifically for eucharistic themes rather than sacrificial themes. I can now do this from the standpoint of a relatively "pure" understanding of the early Christian concept of sacrifice. For, up to now, I have methodically excluded the "eucharistic question" (i.e., our own systematic and sometimes polemically influenced concerns about church and Eucharist) in order to avoid forcing questions from a later age upon the early material. Until now, discussions of the Eucharist as sacrifice usually began with a pre-formed concept of the Eucharist and used it as an interpretative framework for the sacrificial material. Now we can reverse the process and study the idea of the Eucharist as sacrifice in the order of its actual historical development. Having first formed a concept of Christian sacrifice independently of eucharistic considerations, we can see how helpful this concept is as an interpretative framework for the early Christian eucharistic material.

The intensive, basic research which lies behind this book has been completed only as far as the third century A.D.[2] The completion of this research, God willing, will probably be a lifetime project. The desire to make some of my findings reasonably accessible without delay to a broad readership arose when I began to realize their ecumenical, pastoral, and general religious and theological significance.

---

2. A detailed account of this research can be found in the extensively documented monograph soon to appear: Robert J. Daly, *Christian Sacrifice: The Judaeo-Christian Background before Origen* (Studies in Christian Antiquity 18; Washington: The Catholic University of America Press, 1978) 587 pp. (CS).

CHAPTER ONE

INTRODUCTION

THE MEANING OF THE WORD "SACRIFICE"[1]

Some words are highly flexible in meaning, especially when they pass from one age or culture to another. Outside academic circles, "doctor," which originally meant scholar or teacher (early translations of Luke 2:46 have Jesus sitting among the "doctors" in the temple), now usually refers to a physician who, originally, was not called a doctor at all. This flexibility is also common in religious language. The word "spiritual," for example, can mean "religious," or "mystical," or "nonmaterial," or "intellectual," or simply the opposite of worldly or secular, or any combination of such meanings. In religious language, the word "sacrifice" (and its synonyms and cognates) has a long history which endows it with a variety of meanings from both the secular and the religious spheres.

The popular use of the word sacrifice is very often wholly secular.

> [It] describes some sort of renunciation, usually destruction, of something valuable in order that something more valuable may be obtained. One may sacrifice duty for pleasure or pleasure for duty, or honesty for gain or gain for honesty. One may sacrifice an eye or a limb or a life for one's country or for some other country. One may even sell stocks "at a sacrifice."[2]

1. For much of the material in this section I am particularly indebted to R. K. Yerkes, *Sacrifice in Greek and Roman Religions and Early Judaism* (New York: Scribner's, 1952/London: A. & C. Black, 1953) 1–7.
2. Ibid., p. 2.

These modern, secular connotations can be analyzed further: 1) The thing sacrificed may be material (money, a limb) or immaterial (pleasure, fidelity, honor). 2) It must be of some value to the one making the sacrifice. 3) The sacrifice is constituted by the sacrificer *renouncing* or *giving up* the valuable thing of which he or she is henceforth deprived. 4) The sacrifice is *by* somebody, *of* something, and *for* something, but never *to* anybody; it is only a coincidence if the thing sacrificed comes into someone else's possession. 5) Because of the deprivation factor, sacrifice always denotes sadness or misfortune; it is to be avoided, if possible, or at least kept as small as possible. 6) Because one wants to obtain as much as possible for as little as possible, one often compares the cost of the sacrifice with the value of the good obtained. 7) The good for which the sacrifice is made is higher in value than what is sacrificed. (E.g., the baseball batter "gives up" his chance for a crowd-pleasing hit in order to enhance his team's chance of winning.) If the one sacrificing happens to share in the boon, we think of him/her as particularly fortunate. In the "supreme sacrifice" the one sacrificing gives up everything and obtains, for himself at least, nothing. 8) In some usages the meaning is totally negative; no recompense is received or higher value served by the deprivation, as in the Germanic languages when the word *Opfer* (sacrifice, offering) is used of the victim of an accident or criminal assault.

These popular secular concepts of sacrifice so completely dominate modern usage that many people, presuming that they reflect the original meaning of the term, use them to interpret the meaning of sacrifice in ancient religions, in the Old Testament, and in the New Testament sacrifice of Jesus. This has led to massive distortions, especially in certain theories of the atonement, in the Christian understanding both of Christ's sacrifice and of the way in which the individual Christian's participation in that sacrifice is conceived.

In contrast to these predominantly negative connotations in the modern popular use of the term sacrifice, certain other much more positive common features characterize sacrifice in the Semitic-Hebrew (and also Greco-Roman) civilization: 1) The words describing sacrifice generally have no secular significance whatever; they describe strictly religious rites and objects. 2) These words generally connote not reluctance, sadness, or deprivation, but joy, festivity, or thanksgiving; sacrifices usually are performed gladly as expressions of the attitudes of human beings to their God or gods. 3) Proper sacrifices are always as large as possible; the larger the sacrifice the greater the accompanying joy or festivity. 4) Sacrifices are offered *by* men *to* their God (or gods). The stress is upon the *giving*, not on the giving up. 5) Sacrifices are offered both to procure boons and to express thinksgiving for boons received. 6) In Old Testament animal sacrifice, the death of the animal is only a necessary prerequisite or condition for the sacrificial action. *No significance is attached to the death of the animal. Its death, in itself, effects nothing.* Ignorance of this has been the point of departure for some very common but erroneous explanations of sacrifice, that is, those theories of sacrificial atonement which emphasize the suffering and death of the victim or the destruction of the material being offered. Those theories, which raise serious theological problems, are in this respect totally without scriptural foundation.

The contrast between the ancient (biblical) and modern (secular) concepts of sacrifice can be shown as follows:

	ANCIENT	MODERN
Field of use	Wholly religious, never secular	Almost wholly secular; used religiously by transference
Purpose	Solely a cultic act	Never a cultic act
Size of the sacrifice	As large as possible	As small as possible
Recipient	Always offered *to* a god, thus indicating a recognition of superiority	Never offered *to* anyone
Performance and accompanying emotions	Always performed with joy; came to be identified with thanksgiving	Always performed with regret accompanied with sadness
Significant emphasis	Emphasis on giving and action. Deprivation, while a necessary fact, as with all giving, is never a constituent factor of the sacrifice	Emphasis always on giving *up*, and on deprivation

3

	ANCIENT	MODERN
Death, or destruction of the thing sacrificed	Wholly incidental and never with any inherent or significant meaning, a fact, but never a factor in the sacrifice.	Signifies the "supreme sacrifice," a necessary factor in all sacrifice.

GENERAL THEORY OF SACRIFICE[3]

Since the late nineteenth century flowering of the disciplines of history of religions or comparative religion, we have seen numerous energetic attempts to isolate or abstract the *essential idea* common to all sacrifice; that is, what element in the idea of sacrifice is the *primary element* (it is usually presumed that there is a primary element) from which the numerous forms and concepts derive? The most common suggestions for this primary element have been: 1) the *gift* of the human being to the deity, or 2) the *homage* of the subject to the lord, or 3) the *expiation* of offenses, or 4) *communion* with the deity, especially in the sacrificial banquet, or 5) *life* released from the victim, transmitted to the deity, and conferred upon the worshipers.

However, even in a relatively well-defined group like the Old Testament Hebrews, the practice of sacrifice is too complicated for reduction to a single radical element.[4]

For example, one major aspect of Israel's religious and cultural background is its nomadic experience. The sacrificial offering of a nomad is naturally something from his flocks, usually a lamb or a goat. A nomad feels close to the animals in his flocks; they share his existence and his struggle for life in the inhospitable desert. The nomad is also aware that his animals share with him the same life-principle bestowed on them by the deity. Thus it is only natural that the communion and life concepts of sacrifice seem to dominate in Israel's nomadic background. This seems

3. Of the many things written on this subject, one of the most perceptive and readily intelligible is G. B. Gray, *Sacrifice in the Old Testament. Its Theory and Practice* (Oxford: Clarendon, 1925).

4. Cf. J. McKenzie, "Sacrifice," in *Dictionary of the Bible* (Milwaukee: Bruce, 1965) 754.

to be confirmed by the findings of history and archaeology which indicate that the holocaust form of sacrifice (the burning up of the whole sacrificial animal) was not practiced among the early Semitic nomads. An animal was too sacred and valuable to be disposed of in this way. In early communion and life sacrifices the animal (except for the blood, and perhaps also the liver, kidneys, and intestinal fat) was totally eaten, probably in the manner still practiced in the celebrations of the desert bedouin today.[5]

However, another major aspect of Israel's cultural background is agricultural. Many Jews were descendants not of the desert wanderers but of the sedentary Canaanite tillers of the soil who were gradually assimilated into Jewish life and religion after the settlement. The offering of a farmer is not taken from a flock but from the fruits of the earth. In this context, the *gift* and *homage* ideas of sacrifice tend to dominate. The sacrifices of Cain and Abel (Gen 4:3–7) illustrate the difference between the sacrifices of the nomad and the farmer, while also suggesting the tension that often existed between them.

These examples by no means exhaust the considerable variety in Israel's cultural and religious background. Only at the price of oversimplification might one find a clearly dominant central idea in Old Testament sacrifice. Nevertheless, if any idea is basic or central in ancient Israel's practice of sacrifice as presented in the Old Testament, it is the *gift* idea. And what was given or offered in sacrifice, whether from the field or the flock, was some form of food or drink.

In some of the more primitive stages (remains of which can be found in the account of Noah's sacrifice in Gen 8:20ff.), food was given to the gods for them to eat. (Cf. the second century B.C. Jewish polemic against this belief in the story of Bel and the Dragon related in Dan 14.) Traces of this crassly anthropomorphic and materialistic view of sacrifice can be found in some older layers of the Bible. But the Old Testament actually por-

5. See especially W. Robertson Smith, *Lectures on the Religion of the Semites. The Fundamental Institutions* (3d ed., with an Introduction and Additional Notes by S. A. Cook; London: A. & C. Black, 1927 [1st ed., 1889; repr. New York: Schocken, 1973]).

trays (if one can interpret the brush strokes correctly) the gradual purification or elevation or "spiritualization" (see below) of the idea of sacrifice. An example of this is the development of the phrase "pleasing odor—appeasing fragrance—sweet odor" (Gen 8:21) into a technical term signifying the acceptability of sacrifice in God's eyes, an acceptability which is due not to the material richness of the sacrifice but to the proper (internal or spiritual) dispositions of the one offering the sacrifice.

The highest, or most purely "spiritualized," expression of this gift-theory of sacrifice from the pre-Christian Jewish tradition is found in the works of Philo of Alexandria (ca. 13 B.C. to A.D. 45/50). There we find a mature expression of the idea that a sacrifice is only a returning to God of what he has first given us; that it is not *what* we give that is of primary importance, but rather the *dispositions* with which we give; and that ultimately the only gift (or sacrifice) worthy of God is that of a pure mind and soul offering itself to God. Thus, much of what Philo had to say about sacrifice gives witness to the spiritual and spiritualizing developments in late Old Testament and early rabbinic Judaism which formed the foundation of the primitive Christian theology of sacrifice.[6]

THE CONCEPT "SPIRITUALIZATION"

Since any Christian theology of sacrifice involves coming to terms with the spiritualization of sacrifice and its terminology, some clarification of the meaning of this term is needed.

Spiritualization is a term so open to different and even opposing meanings that it can hardly be defined adequately, let alone be represented by a few synonyms. *Dematerializing, sublimating, humanizing, deepening, ethicizing, rationalizing, interiorizing, symbolizing* are some of its commonly used synonyms.[7] But no one of these is adequate, and some of them, such as "dematerializing," can be dangerously misleading. A person, for example,

6. See below, Chap. Five, for a detailed treatment of Philo.

7. Cf. A. Bertholet, *Der Sinn des kultischen Opfers* (Abhandlungen der preussischen Akademie der Wissenschaften, 1942; Phil. hist. Kl. No. 2; Berlin: 1942) 26–27.

who has a rationalistic approach to comparative religions, and who believes that cultic worship is imperfect to the extent that it is material, and that worship approaches perfection to the extent that it has been freed of material elements, will naturally tend to think of sacrifice in terms of a radical dematerializing of it. But this meaning of spiritualization is at odds both with the New Testament and with the incarnational thinking of the founding Fathers of Christian theology—Paul, Barnabas, Irenaeus, Hippolytus, and the two Clements, as we will see below in chapters Four and Five. Thus it cannot be the meaning we attribute to the term in this study.

We are using the word spiritualization in a much broader sense than simply antimaterialistic. This sense includes all those movements and tendencies within Judaism and Christianity which attempted to emphasize the true meaning of sacrifice, that is, the inner, spiritual, or ethical significance of the cult over against the merely material or merely external understanding of it. We include here such different things as: the effort among pious Jews to make their material sacrifice an expression of an ethically good life; the prophetic criticism of the sacrificial cult; the philosophically influenced doubts about the sense of offering material sacrifice to a spiritual God; the necessity of finding substitutes for material sacrifice when participation in the sacrificial cult of the Jerusalem temple was not possible, as in Qumran, or in the diaspora, or after the destruction of the temple. And of course we also include especially the various practices in the areas of cult and worship, in which Christians understood that the old economy of salvation had been superseded by the new.

All these phenomena of spiritualization had in common a shift in emphasis from the material to the spiritual. But their attitudes varied greatly, ranging from Philo's typically Platonic disesteem of things material to the incarnational thought of the Christians who could never, even in their most Platonizing moments, forget that God had come to them in the flesh and that they, in turn, as Paul put it, are called to offer their *bodies* as spiritual worship (Rom 12:1). Thus, when we use the words spiritualize or spiritualization, we are using them—unless otherwise noted—in the very broad sense just explained, not in the narrowly antimaterial, anti-institutional sense usually ascribed to it by the liberal history-of-religions school.[8]

CHRISTIAN SACRIFICE

In order to present as unambiguously as possible the central perspective of this study, we will sketch in advance some of its major conclusions. The concept of Christian sacrifice naturally centers in the person and on the life and teaching of Jesus Christ. After a thorough study of the New Testament and early Christian writings we are able to distinguish therein three main aspects of the Christian theology of sacrifice: 1) the sacrifice of Christ, 2) the sacrifice of the Christian, 3) the Christian(s) as the new temple.

From the very beginning, as the New Testament indicates, Christians looked upon the life and especially the death and resurrection of Jesus as a sacrificial event. Secondarily, they looked upon their own Christian lives as a sharing in, or as an imitation or following of the sacrifice of Christ. At the same time, drawing upon religious ideas already present in Judaism, especially in Qumran, Christians began to look upon the individual and/or the Christian community as the new temple, that is, as the place where the sacrifices of the new covenant are offered.

---

8. Somewhat affected by this antimaterial bias is the very work still regarded by most as the authoritative study on this concept: H. Wenschke-witz, "Die Spiritualisierung der Kultusbegriffe. Tempel, Priester und Opfer im Neuen Testament," *Angelos* 4 (1932) 70–230. A corrective, showing that the process of spiritualization was not exclusively a late, Hellenistically influenced development, but that it goes back well into the biblical period, especially in the Psalms, was supplied by H. J. Hermisson, *Sprache und Ritus im altisraelitischen Kult: Zur "Spiritualisierung" der Kultbegriffe im Alten Testament* (WMANT 19; Neukirchen-Vluyn: Neukirchener Verlag, 1965). See also R. E. Clements, *God and Temple: The Idea of the Divine Presence in Ancient Israel* (Philadelphia: Fortress, 1965; Oxford: Blackwell, 1965) esp. chap. 7 on the Priestly reinterpretation of the cult. This was in fact a form of spiritualization which Clements calls a " 'theologizing' of the cult" (p. 121); and B. Gärtner, *The Temple and Community in Qumran and the New Testament* (SNTS; Cambridge: University Press, 1965) esp. chap. 3: "The 'New Temple' in Qumran" (pp. 16–46).

This sketch of the Christian theology of sacrifice, clearly present in the New Testament, especially in Paul, represents the culmination of a massive transformation or spiritualization of the idea of sacrifice. For the concept of Christian sacrifice in New Testament Christianity was, as we will be able to show, not primarily a cultic or liturgical concept. It was primarily ethical, centered in and growing out of the practical, down-to-earth, everyday experience of Christian life and preaching. This conclusion is powerfully supported by the following more than coincidental facts: There are five texts in the New Testament which say or begin to say something about the meaning or theology of Christian sacrifice. All of these texts, without exception, are found either in or closely associated with passages of exhortation to the practical, diaconal, and ministerial works of the Christian life.[9]

It is obviously inappropriate to start discussing the ramifications of conclusions for which I have not yet properly argued. But it is not out of place to highlight here the importance of the question being raised and the significance of the answer being given. The question of the Eucharist as sacrifice and the concept of the relationship between faith and works have fiercely divided the Christian community since the sixteenth century. On the question of the Eucharist as sacrifice, the Lutheran and Roman Catholic theological communities have now come to a remarkable degree of agreement.[10] As the theological discussions at the 1976 Philadelphia Eucharistic Congress (August 3–5) and the contributions to *The Eucharist in Ecumenical Dialogue*[11] show, the idea of the Eucharist as sacrifice is increasingly one

9. These texts are: Rom 12:1–2; 15:15–16; 1 Pet 2:1–10; Heb 10:19–25; 12:18–13:16. They are given a detailed treatment below in Chap. Four.

10. Cf. *Lutherans and Catholics in Dialogue III: The Eucharist as Sacrifice*, published jointly by representatives of the U.S.A. National Committee of the Lutheran World Federation and the Bishop's Committee for Ecumenical and Interreligious Affairs (New York: U.S.A. National Committee for Lutheran World Federation/Washington: U.S. Catholic Conference, 1967). See esp. pp. 188–91.

11. L. Swidler, ed., *The Eucharist in Ecumenical Dialogue*, a special issue of the *Journal of Ecumenical Studies* 13:2 (1976) 91–344.

which unites Christians, at least for discussion, rather than divides them.

Much of this agreement, however, remains terminological. For it has not yet been clearly demonstrated precisely what was the concept of sacrifice operative in the New Testament church and in the communities of the first few centuries. These were the Christians who first spoke and wrote, allusively at first, and then increasingly clearly, of the Eucharist as sacrifice. Now, liberated from the polemics of the Reformation and Counter-Reformation which condemned us to read into the remote past the concepts and biases of a more recent past, we are able at last to examine this phenomenon more clearly and to allow the realities of the Christ-event and early Christian life to speak challengingly on their own terms to our contemporary concepts and biases.

Some clearer insight into the relationship between faith and works is also made possible by this study. As we take cognizance of the way in which the New Testament and early church looked upon Christian life as spiritualized sacrifice, it becomes clear to us that the operative concept of sacrifice in the New Testament is primarily ethical and we are brought to a new awareness of a harmonious integration between faith and works which we have tended to neglect in our own polemically conditioned discussions. In this, and in other ways which the reader will discover, we hope that this study can help bring about such an understanding that the word and concept "sacrifice" or "Christian sacrifice" might never again become a scandalous cause of argument among Christians, and that, instead, it might prove to be a vital impetus toward increasing unity in Christ.

CHAPTER TWO

THE OLD TESTAMENT

THE PROBLEM AND THE METHOD

Most of the Old Testament was written down in various stages between the years 1000 and 100 B.C. It is thus obvious that one must at least ask the question about the reliability of these writings as historical sources for events which, in some cases, took place long before they were written down (the patriarchal and Exodus stories), and, in other cases, even before the beginning of recorded history (the creation stories and the "prehistory" of Gen 1–11).

The problems uncovered by this question become vastly more complicated when we recall that the Old Testament, especially the Pentateuch (first five books), underwent multiple revisions in which the thinking and attitudes of later periods were projected back into the stories and accounts of earlier periods. For example, the first seven chapters of Leviticus codify the ritual prescriptions for sacrifice. Although these laws are presented as coming from the mouth of Moses, they are actually the product of a relatively late redactional process which had many levels and which culminated in the activity of the post-exilic Priestly writers of the fourth or fifth century B.C.—almost one thousand years after the time of Moses. Most scholars agree that Leviticus projects the theology and concerns of these post-exilic Priestly writers back into the time and the mouth of Moses.

We have still only scratched the surface of the question of how the Old Testament was written. For the Priestly writers (P) were but one of at least four readily distinguishable schools of writers responsible for the early historical books of the Old Testament.

The Yahwist (*J*), so called because he uses the name Yahweh (German: *Jahwe*) for the God of Israel, wrote around the time of Solomon in the tenth century B.C. He gave us the vivid story of the creation and fall of Adam and Eve in Genesis 2–3 and the Noah saga in Genesis 8. One of his main purposes was apparently to present Israel's salvation-history as leading up to a high point in the establishment of the royal house of David. The Elohist (*E*), so called because he uses the name *El* for the God of Israel, wrote a bit later, in the ninth century B.C. We owe to him important parts of the Abraham saga such as the covenant between God and Abraham (Gen 15) and the sacrifice of Isaac (Gen 22). He represents the Northern Kingdom of Israel after the post-Solomonic break of these ten northern tribes with Benjamin and Judah. He thus presents a historical and theological picture distinct from and sometimes in tension with that of the Yahwist. The Deuteronomists (*D*) of the late pre-exilic age (seventh century B.C.) not only gave us Deuteronomy but also, during and after the sixth century exile, gathered and edited most of the extensive historical material we find in the books of Judges, Samuel, and Kings. They update the law and illustrate in Israel's history the working out of the covenant theology implicitly present in the Elohist and vigorously preached by the written prophets. However, all that has survived from these writers has passed through the censoring hands of the post-exilic Priestly writers (*P*) who, with an eye for enhancing the institutional, legal, and ritual significance of the material, not only compiled but also edited the various traditions into the form in which we now know the Old Testament.

Nevertheless, even though we can now reconstruct reasonably well the history of Old Testament sacrifice,[1] the problem remains that no one in Old or New Testament times was aware of this

---

1. *CS*, 1–207; R. de Vaux, *Ancient Israel: Its Life and Institutions* trans. J. McHugh (2d ed.; London: Darton, Longman & Todd, 1965) 271–571; *Studies in Old Testament Sacrifice* (Cardiff: University of Wales Press, 1964); G. B. Gray, *Sacrifice in the Old Testament: Its Theory and Practice* (Oxford: Clarendon, 1925); R. J. Thompson, *Penitence and Sacrifice in Early Israel outside the Levitical Law* (Leiden: Brill, 1963); R. Rendtorff, *Studien zur Geschichte des Opfers im Alten Israel* (WMANT 24; Neukirchen-Vluyn: Neukirchener Verlag, 1967)

historical development. Usually their only escape from a prima facie literal-historical reading of the sacred traditions was typology or allegory. Although salvation-history interests us more than history as such, nonetheless, for our study modern historical criticism will provide the basic framework and methodological matrix. For this alone will bring order to our attempt to make contact with the theology and salvation-history ideas of those who were themselves innocent of the complexities of historical science even while they were themselves components of a highly complex historical process. This too enables us to trace more surely the actual growth of the idea of sacrifice, thus providing a more solid base for theological analysis and reflection.

We will take up in this chapter the two major types of Old Testament sacrifice, the *burnt offering* and the *sin offering*, giving special attention to the theological significance implicit in their ceremonies and practice. Because of its close association with burnt offering, the theology of divine acceptance will be discussed immediately after that section. Chapter Three will treat some further aspects which are of special significance for the sacrificial theology of the New Testament.

THE BURNT OFFERING OR HOLOCAUST

The burnt offering is the most important and most frequently mentioned type of Old Testament sacrifice. More than any sacrificial rite it fulfilled a broad variety of functions, and it contained or suggested a richness of meaning that exercised great influence on the Christian idea of sacrifice.

Terms such as "burnt offering" or "holocaust" or "offering by fire" refer to sacrifices in which the sacrificial material, usually an animal, sometimes grain, was *wholly* burned on the altar (cf. Lev 1–2). It is distinguished from offerings in which only *part* was burned while the rest was consumed *by the people* (peace or covenant offerings or sacrificial banquets—cf. esp. Lev 3) or *by the priests alone* (the sin and guilt offerings—Lev 4; 5; 6:26– 30; 7:6–10; 10:16–20). It is also distinguished from those in which *none* of the offering was burned, such as first fruits and tithes (usually designated by the term *Corban*—cf. Mk 7:11), set aside for the support of the temple and its personnel.

The *historical origins* of the Israelite burnt offerings are obscure. The most satisfying hypothesis is that a pre-Greek, pre-Semitic people existed in the area south of the Taurus Mountains in southern Turkey. They practiced the sacrificial banquet (*zebaḥ*) and the burnt offering (*'ōlâ*). Eventually they were pushed out or absorbed by the Greeks and Semites who also adopted their sacrificial ceremonies. In this way these rites became well established among the Canaanites (Northwest Semites). The Hebrews subsequently adopted them from the Canaanites at the time of the settlement after Moses and Joshua.[2]

This hypothesis makes sense of the prophetic reproach that Israel did not offer burnt offerings and celebrate sacrificial banquets in the desert (Amos 5:21–25; Jer 7:21–26). The prophets may well have meant something like: "Your fathers in the desert never offered sacrifices *such as these* ceremonies you have adopted from the Canaanites." This is what we would expect from the prophets who were, on the one hand, generally mistrustful of the urban priestly classes with their syncretistic (Canaanite sun-god worship) leanings, but were, on the other hand, generally close to the rural segments of the people who instinctively looked back to the desert wandering as a time of religious purity and closeness to God.[3]

The repeated mention of presettlement burnt offerings in J (Gen 8:20; Exod 10:25) and E (Gen 22:1–14; Exod 24:5; 32:6) as well as in the Book of the Covenant (Exod 20:24) might seem to contradict the view of history we have just suggested until we recall that the literary formulation of these traditions took place after the settlement when a burnt offering ritual similar to that of the Canaanites was already firmly established at the center of

2. Cf. de Vaux, *Ancient Israel*, 440–41; *Studies in OT Sacrifice*, chap. II, iv; L. Rost, "Erwägungen zum israelitischen Brandepfer" (BZAW 77; Berlin: 1958) 178–83; R. K. Yerkes, *Sacrifice in Greek and Roman Religions and Early Judaism* (London: A. & C. Black, 1953) 146–57.

3. Few exegetes continue to hold the once popular opinion that the prophets condemned sacrifice in principle. The texts in which the prophets fiercely criticize the sacrificial cult are relatively few: Isa 1:10–15; Amos 5:21–25; Hos 6:6; Mic 6:6–8; Jer 6:20–21; 7:21–26.

Israel's sacrificial worship. An analysis of the historicizing process of projecting current ritual practice back into the narration of
earlier historical events quickly leaves only Noah's sacrifice
(Gen 8:20–21 [J]) and the sacrifice of Isaac (Gen 22:1–14 [E])
as possible presettlement burnt offerings (see CS, 36–41).

For the account of Noah's sacrifice in Genesis 8, Tablet XI of
the Babylonian Gilgamesh epic is the closest known literary
source:

> Then I [Utnapishtim] let out (all) to the four winds and offered
> a sacrifice.
> I poured out a libation on the top of the mountain.
> Seven and seven cult-vessels I set up,
> Upon their pot-stands I heaped the cane, cedarwood and myrtle.
> The gods smelled the savor,
> The gods smelled the sweet savor,
> The gods crowded like flies about the sacrificer.[4]

The notable differences in the Bible story are that Noah built an
altar, chose clean animals, offered burnt offerings (expressed by
the common Old Testament technical term for burnt offerings).
Most likely this account is not based on a historical reminiscence
of a prehistoric burnt offering. For the West Semitic and
Israelite burnt offering is the one rite known to J which closely
resembles what is described in the Gilgamesh epic. Since this
burnt offering ritual was the highest form of sacrifice known to J
he could hardly have found anything better suited to express the
solemnity of the occasion. Thus Genesis 8 offers no real proof
that presettlement Israel knew and practiced the burnt offering.

Similarly, in the Elohist description of the sacrifice of Isaac
(Gen 22:1–14), we note first of all that the basic elements of the
burnt offering ritual seem to have been consciously chosen to
form the story's framework. The account also agrees closely
with the ritual of another burnt offering from the period in which
E was writing: the sacrifices of Elijah and the prophets of Baal
on Mt. Carmel (1 Kgs 18:20–38). Therefore, without knowledge

---

4. J. B. Pritchard, *Ancient Near Eastern Texts Relating to the Old
Testament* (2d ed.; Princeton: Princeton University Press, 1955) 95.

of the earlier forms of the story of Abraham sacrificing Isaac, and with the knowledge that E clothed this story in the framework of the burnt offering ritual of his own day, we can only conclude that this passage too offers no real proof of presettlement Israelite burnt offerings.[5]

The idea or the theology of the burnt offering is not articulated in the Old Testament sacrificial code which, in fact, does not even prescribe what the worshipers were supposed to be thinking as they offered sacrifice. But the varied functions of the burnt offering contain an implicit theology which we can educe from the texts. It is noteworthy that all three of the most common general theories of sacrifice (gift, communion, propitiation/expiation) are found verified in varying degrees in the different burnt offering rites.

The burnt offering rite was used on the following occasions: 1) The daily burnt offering of one lamb opened the sacrificial service each day—Num 28:6. 2) Additional burnt offerings served as the special sacrifices of feast days—Num 28:1–29:40. 3) It served as a royal sacrifice—especially 2 Kgs 16:15. 4) It served as a purification rite, especially of a mother after childbirth—Leviticus 12. 5) It served as a sacrifice of atonement (see below 25–30), especially in the earlier periods—cf. Leviticus 4; 5; 16. 6) It expressed joy, thanksgiving, and recognition of Yahweh's superiority—Exod 32:6; Judg 6:25–32; 11:29–40; 1 Sam 6:14; 1 Kgs 18:17–40. 7) It served as the private sacrifice of an individual (Lev 1:2–12; Num 15:1–10; Ezek 44:11; 2 Chr 29:31–35; Ezra 3:1–6). Finally the close relationship between the burnt offering and the altar is significant; it at least implied that the main purpose of the altar was to be the place where burnt offerings were sacrificed.

Fire,[6] consumes and vaporizes; it strives to heaven; it makes the smoke go up. How natural it was for primitive man to see

5. See the more extensive treatment below, pp. 47–52, and in R. J. Daly, "The Soteriological Significance of the Sacrifice of Isaac," *CBQ* 39 (1977) 45–75.

6. See CS, 52–61; J. Morgenstern, *The Fire upon the Altar* (Leiden: Brill, 1963).

fire as a means of symbolizing or effecting communion with the deity, or of giving to him his share in the sacrifice. But, in the developed religious consciousness of the Priestly writers, *no ordinary fire would do*; it had to be sacred fire. "Strange fire" (Lev 10:1–2; Num 3:4; 26:21) was strictly forbidden under the severest of penalties. The late Priestly writers also laid great stress on the fact that the fire on the altar is a perpetual fire (Lev 6:8–9, 12–13). Yet Lev 1:7 contradicts this when it speaks of putting fire on the altar; and Num 4:1–16, amid all the detailed instructions for transporting the tabernacle and its varied paraphernalia, does not even mention the fire. In short, the principle of the perpetual sacred fire on the altar seems to have been a postexilic innovation whose history comprises one of the more fascinating aspects of the Old Testament.

Solomon's temple was constructed after the pattern of a North Semitic solar sanctuary (cf. 1 Kgs 5). By this time in the tenth century the solar calendar and at least some of the external trappings of the Phoenician and Canaanite sun cult had been adopted by the Hebrews. The high point of this cult was the annual coming of the *k^ebod Yahweh* (glory of God) at sunrise of the autumnal equinoctial day:

> The first rays of the rising sun would enter through the opened portals of the temple's great eastern gate, pass down the east-west axis of the temple, over the altar of sacrifice causing the sacred fire of that year to enkindle (miraculously?), then on into the sanctuary building, and finally into the *debir*, the Holy of Holies at the western end of the sanctuary whose portals and veils were opened only once a year, at this moment, to receive the Glory of God. For a brief moment, the sun's rays penetrated the innermost recess of the sanctuary and illumined it with golden radiance (cf. Isa. 6:1–10; 60:1). This was originally celebrated as New Year's Day, the most important feast of the year. Upon its proper celebration depended the welfare of the entire nation. After the exile this day came to be observed as the great Day of Atonement (cf. Lev 16), to this day the most solemn holy day of the Jews.[7]

This strongly solar form of the cult with its convenient solar calendar was apparently quite acceptable to the progressive,

7. Summarized from J. Morgenstern, "Biblical Theophanies," *ZA* 25 (1911) 139–93; 28 (1913) 15–60; *The Fire upon the Altar*, 7–8.

commercial, basically urban-oriented party served by the Jerusalem priesthood. But it could not escape challenge from the traditionalist, basically rural-oriented prophetic party which was constantly calling Israel to return to the religious purity it associated with the desert wandering. To them, all these innovations, so blatantly borrowed from the cult of Baal, were an abomination. Much of Old Testament cultic history reflects the tension between these two parties: the ritually progressive, innovative, urban-oriented institutional priesthood as opposed to the ritually conservative, traditional, rural-oriented prophets. (A great deal of Western religious history has often been a tale of similar tensions, for example, institutional office versus individual or private charism.)

A critical turning point in this history of the sacred fire can be located at the post-exilic dedication of the second temple. The glory of Yahweh in its solar manifestation comes again from the east at dawn of the autumnal equinox, but the Priestly author of Ezekiel 40–48 conceives this as happening now, once and for all for the last time. Yahweh will now remain permanently in the temple; no more will the great doors of the eastern gate be opened annually, for the glory of Yahweh will have already entered definitively to take up his abode permanently in the Most Holy Place (Ezek 43:7; 44:2; Hag 1:7–8). The sacred fire would no longer be kindled by the annual coming of the glory of Yahweh; it would have to be kept burning, as the new legislation in Leviticus 6 emphasizes. This was the final nail in the coffin of the old solar cult of Yahweh. It was also not long before the (now continuously burning) fire on the altar came to be looked upon as the same continuously burning fire which came down from heaven at the dedication of Solomon's temple:

> When Solomon had ended his prayer, fire came down from heaven and consumed the burnt offering and the sacrifices, and the glory of the Lord filled the temple. And the priests could not enter the house of the Lord, because the glory of the Lord filled the Lord's house. When all the children of Israel saw the fire come down and the glory of the Lord upon the temple, they bowed down with their faces to the earth on the pavement, and worshiped and gave thanks to the Lord. . . . (2 Chr 7:1–3)

The final stage in this history was the growth of a number of supporting sacred legends relating how the sacred fire was miraculously preserved (for example, in the form of a liquid) between the time of the destruction of the Solomonic temple in 587 B.C. and its restoration some seven or more decades later. Just such a legend is recorded in 2 Macc 1:18–2:10.

The religious significance of the sacred fire was intensely heightened by all these developments. The early Israelites shared with other primitive peoples a sacred awe of fire. It was a connecting link between heaven and earth, a means of "giving" something to God or of removing it from profane use. It was also a particular way in which God revealed himself to humans, as we can see in Abraham's covenant sacrifice (Gen 15), in the burning bush (Exod 3:1–6) and subsequent Sinai theophanies, in the sacrifices of Gideon (Judg 6:19–24) and Manoah (Judg 13:15–20) and in Elijah's sacrifice on Mt. Carmel (1 Kgs 18:30–40). Fire was not just the symbol but sometimes even the mode of God's presence, as in the descent of the glory of the Lord on Sinai (Exod 19:16–24; 24:15–18) and its subsequent entrance into the tabernacle (Exod 40:34–38). The Hebrews tended to see the presence of God in the fire on the altar, and, as Isaiah's vision (6:1–7) shows, the altar itself as the throne of Yahweh. This passage also illustrates the purifying and sanctifying power of the sacred fire (see also 1 Kgs 8:10–11; 2 Chr 5:14; 7:2). Finally, the glory of the Lord could also be a sign and instrument of God's displeasure (Exod 16:7–10). Fire could come forth from the presence of the Lord and devour the wicked (Lev 10:2; Num 16:35). If the *kebod Yahweh* were approached without the proper qualifications and precautions, the result could be equally fatal (cf. Lev 16:13).

Although the *incense offering* (see CS, 64–69) played a minor role in the overall history of Israelite sacrifice (archaeologists cannot agree on whether Solomon's temple even had an altar of incense), by New Testament times it had acquired a religious significance that made it, in terms of later theological developments, one of the most important of Old Testament sacrificial rites. The offering of incense was a gesture of homage to the

Lord God; hence the appropriateness, on the one hand, of the gift of the Magi and, on the other hand, of the adamant Christian refusal to offer incense to the emperor. The Israelites came to attribute extraordinary powers to the incense offering: it was effective not only for obtaining Yahweh's good graces and for making atonement for the people (Num 16:46–50), but also for protection against the deadly force of the Lord's presence when the high priest entered the Holy of Holies on Yom Kippur (Lev 16:13). Understandably, abuse of incense was considered a most serious offense with dire consequences for the offender (Lev 10:1–2; Num 3:4; 26:61).

In New Testament times incense was burned as part of the morning and evening continual burnt offering (*'ōlâ tamîd*). The morning incense offering was the most solemn part of the daily ritual. All waited silently while the priest, chosen by lot, entered the Holy Place to offer incense on the golden altar. It was as if the life of the nation hung suspended until the clouds of incense billowed forth from the Holy Place to signal the psalmists to start chanting and the sacrificing priests to begin offering the lamb of the *tamîd*. This was the setting for Zechariah's vision in Luke 1:8–21. It was also apparently central in the imagination of the author of Revelation:

> When the Lamb opened the seventh seal, there was silence in heaven for about half an hour. Then I saw the seven angels who stand before God, and seven trumpets were given to them. And another angel came and stood at the altar with a golden censer; and he was given much incense to mingle with the prayers of all the saints upon the golden altar before the throne; and the smoke of the incense rose with the prayers of the saints from the hand of the angel before God. (Rev 8:1–4)

> And when he had taken the scroll, the four living creatures and the twenty-four elders fell down before the Lamb, each holding a harp, and with golden bowls full of incense, which are the prayers of the saints. . . . (Rev 5:8)

The identification of "the prayers of the saints" with incense doubtless alludes to the much-quoted Ps 141:2: "Let my prayer be counted as incense before thee, and the lifting up of my hands as an evening sacrifice!"

Thus it is easy to see how the minds and imaginations of those who meditated on the meaning of the sacrificial customs could fasten on the incense offering. Its interpretation played an important part in the development of a spiritualized idea of sacrifice in the early church. In the third century Origen repeatedly quotes Ps 141:2 to express his idea of Christian life as sacrificial.

One reason why the idea of life itself as sacrificial became so popular with early Christian writers was the way Philo of Alexandria, two centuries earlier, had contrasted the crude altar of sacrifice set in the open air with the precious altar of incense set inside the Holy Place. As Philo put it:

> This clearly shows that even the least morsel of incense offered by a man of religion is more precious in the sight of God than thousands of cattle sacrificed by men of little worth. . . . The symbolic meaning is just this and nothing else: that what is precious in the sight of God is not the number of victims immolated but the true purity of a rational spirit in him who makes the sacrifice. (*de Specialibus Legibus* I 274–77)

THE DIVINE ACCEPTANCE OF SACRIFICE

The theology of the divine acceptance of sacrifice (see *CS*, 70–84), although pertinent to all sacrifice, had a development which particularly associated it with burnt offerings. The value or effectiveness of any sacrifice was perceived as being dependent wholly on its being accepted by Yahweh. (He who accepts a gift is bound by particular ties of favor to the donor—cf. the reconciliation scene between Jacob and Esau in Gen 33:9–11.) The most important technical term signifying that an offering and its offerer are pleasing and acceptable to God is the phrase *rêaḥ niḥōaḥ*—"soothing odor," "pleasing fragrance," "odor of sweetness." Its original, anthropomorphic sense was that the deity was literally placated by the sweet fragrance of the burning sacrifice. Traces of this primitive meaning remain in Noah's sacrifice (Gen 8:21) and in David's perplexed question/complaint to King Saul who had been trying to kill him: "If it is the Lord who has stirred you up against me, may he smell a sacrifice" (1 Sam 26:19).[8]

Outside of these two cases, *rêaḥ nîḥōaḥ* (RSV: pleasing odor) is used in the Old Testament some forty times, but only metaphorically in the relatively late Priestly texts, as a technical term signifying God's acceptance of a sacrifice and the one(s) offering it. Interestingly, P does not use this phrase in an expiatory or atoning sense (for this he uses *kipper* or "atonement" as we shall see below). It is probable that the Priestly writers were no longer aware of the physically realistic meaning of the phrase. It is clear, in any case, that for them the phrase expressed primarily the higher religious sentiments of self-giving devotion, of praise, adoration, or thanksgiving.

Christians too have used this phrase in precisely the same sense. Many formulas of religious profession or ordination include the petition that "the Lord accept this holocaust (of the vows and religious life) in an odor of sweetness." It is regrettable that the elimination of archaic language in the updating of these vow formulas has sometimes also eliminated the notion of sacrificial self-giving which expresses the essence of the Christian life as an imitation of Christ the Servant who emptied himself for us.[9]

A further development of this Old Testament theology comes, unexpectedly, from a translation: the Septuagint.[10] The Greek translators took pains to avoid the suggestion, which the Hebrew text itself might easily give, that "pleasing odor" is a real substantive signifying something objectively valid in the sacrifice itself.[11] In this late Old Testament context the phrase seems to express these two important things about the function and purpose of sacrifice: 1) God's acceptance of the sacrifice is a totally free act.

8. "Smell a sacrifice" is indeed a literal rendering of the Hebrew. This suggests how primitive (or physically realistic) the religious sentiments of the historical David probably were. Modern translators (e.g., RSV: "accept an offering") usually translate the phrase metaphorically rather than literally.

9. A recent discussion of this problem can be found in Hans Küng, *On Being a Christian,* trans. E. Quinn (New York: Doubleday, 1976) 424–27.

10. See also below, pp. 36–37.

11. See S. Daniel, *Recherches sur le vocabulaire du culte dans la Septante* (Etudes et Commentaires 61; Paris: C. Klincksieck, 1966) 176, 186–97.

God is "bound" to accept from humans only to the extent that he freely chooses. 2) The sacrifice is, nevertheless, somehow expected to "make an impression" or "arouse an effect" in God. The apparent contradiction is the same as the paradox implicit in prayer: the belief that prayer is efficacious before God, but that God still remains transcendent and immutable.

This "theology of acceptance" pervades Old Testament attitudes toward sacrifice. A particularly notable instance of it comes from the tenth century B.C. Yahwist:

> And the Lord had regard for Abel and his offering, but for Cain and his offering he had no regard. So Cain was angry and his countenance fell. The Lord said to Cain, "Why are you angry, and why has your countenance fallen? If you do well, will you not be accepted?" (Gen 4:4–7)

The divine acceptance is not seen as automatic; God is free to accept or reject the offering. It is also clear that everything depends on God's acceptance; nonacceptance is a disaster, although not necessarily the ultimate rejection. Further, acceptance of the offering is implicitly identified with favorable acceptance of the offerer. Finally, implicit to the whole passage is the idea, later preached so forcefully by the prophets, that the good conduct and intentions of the offerer are of paramount importance.

The prophets, far from totally rejecting sacrifice, as has often been assumed, actually provide further striking proof of the pervasiveness of this sacrificial theology of acceptance. Their fierce denunciations of sacrifice make use of the cultic technical terms which signify divine acceptance or rejection. Phrases such as "Your burnt offerings are not acceptable" (Jer 6:20) or "They shall not please him with their sacrifices" (Hos 9:4) or "I will not accept them" (Amos 5:22) are actually negative formulations of precisely the same ritual formulas which the priests in the temple used to declare that a given sacrifice was being offered properly and was therefore accepted by God. Thus the very criticism of the prophets makes sense only on the supposition that they believed not only in the idea of sacrifice but also in its practical efficacy. Deep in the Old Testament, therefore, we find clear witness to one of the basic points of a mature theology of sacrifice: what really counts is not the material size of the offering but the dispositions of the offerer.

There is, of course, ample evidence that in the Old Testament as elsewhere practice lagged considerably behind the ideal. But this theology is indisputably a genuine Old Testament and pre-Christian achievement, and it was actually carried out at least by some, as can be seen from this incident narrated about Simeon the Just at the beginning of the Christian era:

> Simeon the Just stated that he had never eaten of the guilt-offering of the defiled Nazirite, and only once he had no hesitation to do so. It was when a Nazirite from the Darom came to the Temple to have his hair shaved; he had beautiful eyes, was of good looks and had magnificent curls. "I asked him, My son, what made thee undertake to destroy thy beautiful hair?" He replied, "I was in my town my father's shepherd, and when I one day went to draw water from a well and saw mine image in the water, my impulse seized me and strove to drive me out from the world; but I said, Thou, wicked, why boastest thou of what is not thine and will once turn into maggots and worms? I swear that I shall cut thee off in honor of God!" I kissed him on his head, and said to him, My son, may many like thee be Nazirites in Israel.[12]

Late in the Old Testament period, the theology of acceptance underwent one further development of great import for the later Christian theology of sacrifice. Sacrifice came to be looked on less and less as the ritual performance of an external act and more and more under the precise aspect of an act of obedience to the will of Yahweh.[13] This was the coming-to-term of a spiritualizing process in which observance of the law and other acts of piety could take their place as being of equal religious value beside cultic sacrifice, especially when (for example, in the diaspora or at Qumran) one could not participate in the temple sacrifices. This not only made it possible for the religion of

12. A. Büchler, *Studies in Sin and Atonement in the Rabbinic Literature of the First Century* (Library of Biblical Studies; New York: KTAV, 1967; original ed. 1928) 419.

13. W. Eichrodt, *Theology of the Old Testament* (2 vols.; Philadelphia: Westminster, 1961–67; London: SCM, 1961–67) 1. 168–72.

Judaism to survive the loss of its temple; it also established a theological principle by which Christians could look upon the various activities of Christian living, and the Christian life itself, as sacrificial.

SIN OFFERING AND ATONEMENT

The concepts of sin and atonement (see *CS*, 87–138),[14] or at least the reality or experiences addressed by these concepts, are central to the attempt of Jew and Christian to make sense of their origin, their experience, and their destiny. But even within Christianity, the understanding of sin has not been univocal; and Christianity's theories of atonement can even be described as variegated. Our purpose here will be to sketch out, in as historically objective a way as possible, the Old Testament understanding of the concepts of sin and atonement. For when we find in subsequent history or in our own time an understanding of these concepts which is internally inconsistent with what one perceives to be genuinely Christian, the primary historical question must become our first point of inquiry.

The concept of atonement which we have found to be central to the Old Testament can be described as the process whereby the creature-Creator relationship, after having been disturbed (by the creature), is restored by the Creator to its proper harmony. After the Exile, this atoning process came to be associated with one type of sacrifice, the sin offering, and especially with a particular part of that sacrifice, the blood rite. For it was the ritual manipulation of sacrificial blood that revealed the cause, or at least the occasion, of atonement in the Old Testament. Even though the Old Testament says nothing of the meaning of *kipper* or atonement, with the possible exception of Lev 17:11, 14 and Gen 9:4, it remains possible to educe from the uses of *kipper* a genuine Old Testament theology of atonement.

14. I am dependent, in general, on the line of interpretation proposed by G. von Rad, *Old Testament Theology*, trans. D. M. G. Stalker (2 vols.; New York: Harper & Row, 1962–65) 1. 262–72. Von Rad's insights are given a brilliant philosophical and cultural amplification in P. Ricoeur, *The Symbolism of Evil*, trans. E. Buchanan (New York: Harper & Row, 1967).

The verb *kipper* (etymologically: to cover), sixty-nine of whose ninety-one instances are in P, means basically *to carry out an atoning action.* What then is Israel's idea of sin or of the condition or situation remedied by *kipper?* Sin was an offense or flagrant act (whether or not the subject was aware of its sinfulness) against a sacred ordinance, hence against God and his majesty. It could occur in all phases of life and was by nature a social reality, never strictly private. It was thought that thereby an evil had been set loose which, unless atoned for, would return to plague the individual and/or his community or children. For ancient Israel conceived of itself as a holy camp surrounded by a massive, threatening evil force. A transgression, any act needing atonement, would set in motion some of this evil which, if not neutralized by atonement, would eventually set loose its destructive force on the land and its people.

Behind this is an intensely *synthetic* view of life in which there is the closest possible correspondence between a deed and its consequences and between the temple and the land and the people. Coupled with this is a *pervasive* materiality in ancient Israel's idea of the holy. Israel never gave up conceiving of holiness (the "pure" and the "clean") and unholiness (the "impure" and the "unclean") in a highly material way. An important consequence of this was the tremendous *contagious* or *contaminating* power of evil. The inevitable result of contact was that the pure, the holy, or the clean was made impure, unholy, unclean. Some atoning ceremony would then have to be performed to enable the contaminated person or object to return to its proper position of favor in the eyes of God.

Precisely here Christianity made one of its most significant breaks with Judaism. Christ quite consciously turned this contaminating one-way street into a two-way street in which the holy has power to sanctify the unholy. He healed on the sabbath, insisted that his disciples were "blameless" when plucking grain on the sabbath, even allowed a prostitute to touch him, unafraid of contamination but confident that his holiness could sanctify her. He was not afraid to make physical—hence "defiling"—contact with the leprous and the dead, aware that the life within him is stronger than any evil. St. Paul grasped this; although he was characteristically Jewish in warning against contamination by intercourse with a prostitute, he was characteristically Christian in teaching that the non-Christian marriage partner does not contaminate but rather is sanctified by marital union with his/her Christian spouse (cf. 1 Cor 7:12–16).

Finally, the religious psychology of Judaism at the end of the Old Testament period was characterized by an intensely heightened awareness on the one hand of the transcendent holiness and total otherness of God and on the other hand of the abject frailty and sinfulness of the human condition. The anthropomorphic but intimate familiarity of man with God in the Abraham stories gave way to the idea of a God so transcendent that intermediaries (angels, elaborate ritual, etc.) were needed for the sinful creature to approach the Creator even with fear and trembling. This awareness of transcendence combined with Israel's historical experience of its own sinfulness to produce in the Jewish religious consciousness of Christ's time a profound awareness of the need for atonement. This accounts for the late rise to prominence of a particular sacrificial ceremony suited to this need: the *sin offering*. Not only in the late Old Testament but also in the New Testament, the sin offering and the ideas of forgiveness and atonement associated with it have come to the forefront.

The *process of atonement* had a twofold function: the *positive* function of making persons or objects "acceptable" to Yahweh, of preserving them in this condition, of making them eligible to participate in Israel's religious life and sacrificial cult; and the *negative*, apotropaic function of interrupting or averting the course of evil set in motion by sin or transgression, whether knowing or unknowing (cf. Lev 10:6; Num 1:53; 17:11; 18:5). The words propitiation, expiation, and forgiveness, often used as general words for the process of atonement, can also refer to specific aspects of this process.[15]

15. Unfortunately, scholarship has yet to agree on a consistent terminology of atonement. The definitions given here have been chosen because they describe the clearly distinguishable aspects of the process of atonement.

Actions of *propitiation* soothe the anger or ill will of the deity and/or secure the deity's favor. This idea originally presupposed a crassly material notion of an arbitrary deity who had to be "bought off" or kept happy. With the growing awareness that the creature cannot exert pressure on the immutable God, this cruder conception tended to give way to the higher religious sentiments of praise, petition, adoration, thanksgiving, and recognition of God's excellence. Propitiation involves the notion of a *God-directed action* of the creature.

Actions of *expiation* put in order between creature and Creator the relationships which had been disturbed by sin or transgression. It is, in contrast to propitiation, a creature-directed action in which ultimately God alone is the subject or agent. Things as well as persons can be the objects of expiation as the Yom Kippur ritual of Leviticus 16 shows.

Forgiveness, in the specific sense, was God's ultimate gift of personal favor which, conceptually at least, follows upon and is thus distinguished from the atoning actions of expiation (cf. Büchler, *Studies in Sin and Atonement,* 461). An example of this is the forgiveness granted to David after repenting of Uriah's murder in 2 Sam 12:13.

However, complete clarification in the terminology will not come easily. For the Old Testament was not wholly consistent in viewing atonement as ultimately a creature-directed action of *God*; and we for our part inherit a long tradition which has usually viewed atonement as a penitential act by which we "earn" or make ourselves worthy of God's forgiveness.

The *sin offering* was developed by the Jerusalem priesthood after the exile into the dominant ritual means of atonement. It has the following distinguishable parts:

1) *Bringing the sacrificial material to the altar:* this was an animal (if the offerers could afford it) which had previously been examined to make sure that it was of the right kind and without blemish.

2) The *laying on of hands,* prescribed for all (except guilt offering) animal sacrifices, apparently entered into the ritual with the sin offering, in particular via the scapegoat ritual of the Yom

Kippur liturgy (Lev 16:21–22). Through a confession spoken by Aaron (see below) as he laid his hands on the head of the goat, the sins of the Israelites were transferred to the scapegoat who bears them away. This rendered them harmless. But this ritual was neither a sin offering nor a sacrifice, for the sin offering for atonement had already taken place before this point in the liturgy. Although we cannot determine precisely how much of the original meaning accompanied the assumption of this ceremony into the ritual of the sin offering and other sacrifices, there is general agreement that the rite of the laying on of hands signifies a certain connection—identification, some would say—between the offerer and the animal victim. Above all, it is essential to note that this rite does not of itself signify the penal substitution of the animal victim in place of the human offerer, although it is easy to understand how this interpretation could become more appealing in the later years of the Old Testament when substitutionary ideas were growing in strength.

3) *Confession:* the Yom Kippur ritual instructs Aaron, while laying hands on the scapegoat's head, to "confess over him all the iniquities of the people of Israel" (Lev 16:21). At the time of Christ at least some kind of "confession" accompanying the sin offering must have been practiced, for the priest had to inquire about the kind of sacrifice—sin offering or thank offering or whatever—that was being brought forward; and if it was a sin or guilt offering the priest had to assure himself that the injury, if any, to one's neighbor was being repaired before he could allow the sacrifice to proceed. That this was not just a grand ideal but was at least sometimes actually realized can be seen from the story about Simeon the Just quoted above. It also provides the obvious background for the dominical saying: "If you are offering your gift at the altar, and there remember that your brother has something against you, leave your gift there before the altar and go; first be reconciled to your brother, and then come and offer your gift" (Matt 5:23–24).

4) This was followed by the *slaughtering* of the victim, performed by the offerer, or, in later times, by Levites or other cultic officials. In the face of some extreme theories of penal substitu-

tion, we can hardly stress enough the fact that *the Old Testament never attached much importance to the slaughtering of the victim.* This was, for the most part, just the necessary means of obtaining sacrificial flesh and, above all, sacrificial blood.

5) *The blood rite:* it was in the cultic manipulation of sacrificial blood that atonement was generally seen to take place (see below).

6) A *declaratory formula* spoken by the priest on behalf of Yahweh affirmed the validity or efficacy of the sacrifice. This signified, on the surface, the priest's judgment that the ritual had been carried out according to the law. On a deeper level it also signified that Yahweh, who is above all faithful and true, accepted the sacrifice and effected the atonement.

7) The *eating by the priests or burning of the flesh* of the sin offering was then carried out in a holy place or "clean place" (Lev 4:12) as the final act of the ritual. For the flesh of the sin offering was considered to be sacred and its disposition in this way was considered to be an essential part of the atoning process, as Lev 10:16–20 and the story about Simeon the Just indicate.

Sacrificial Blood

At the end of the Old Testament, the early rabbinic Judaism out of which Christianity grew tended to attribute an atoning function to every kind of sacrifice, and to associate atonement so closely with the blood rite as practically to identify the two. This strongly influenced primitive Christianity as witnessed by the recurrence in Paul and Revelation of the concept "redeemed in the blood of Christ," and by the fact that the Epistle to the Hebrews is constructed around a christological interpretation of the Day of Atonement blood rite (see below). Hebrews even quotes the popular rabbinic dictum: "without the shedding of blood there is no forgiveness of sins" (Heb 9:22).

Among Israel's neighbors four functions for sacrificial blood are discernible: 1) life-giving or fortifying, 2) cathartic or apotropaic, 3) "sacramental," 4) nutritive. All but the fourth figure also in Israel's cultic history, but comparative religion has been unable to find a highly illuminating parallel for the Old

Testament blood rites. Four Old Testament areas stand out in Israel's use of sacrificial blood: the Exod 24:3–8 covenant sacrifice, the Exodus 12 Passover blood rite, the atonement rituals of Leviticus 4 and 16, and the legislation regarding the use of sacrificial blood (Lev 17:11, 14; Gen 9:4).[16]

Sacrificial blood could be ritually handled in several different ways: by throwing, by pouring it out at the base of the altar, by sprinkling, and by applying or smearing. The last two methods were used in sin offerings (see Lev 4 and 16). Important keys to the meaning of these sin offering blood rites can be found by examining in their apparent chronological order of redactional composition the early Priestly texts of Ezek 43:18–27 and 45:18–20,[17] then the Day of Atonement ritual of Leviticus 16 and the sin offering ritual of Leviticus 4 (later Priestly). This shows that the blood rites of the sprinkling and smearing type seem originally to have had the function of dedicating, consecrating, purifying, atoning for sacred *things*, and then later to have taken on the function of making atonement for *people*.

Summing up, we can say, first, that although the primary purpose of the blood rite in atonement sacrifices was apotropaic, the ultimate goal remained that of rendering both objects and persons eligible to take part in Israel's public life of worship. Secondly, the words "atone," "purify" "consecrate," "shall be forgiven" and their object counterparts "sin," "transgression," "uncleanness" seem to be basically synonymous. Finally, the atoning effect was attributed to the correct performance of the whole rite, but the blood rite was its most important element, the one always mentioned.

Leviticus 17:11 and the Significance of Sacrificial Blood

Only three Old Testament texts, all of them prohibitions against eating blood, even suggest anything about the connection

16. The blood rites of the Passover and covenant sacrifice will be taken up in the following chapter.

17. Ezek 40–48 comes most likely from the hands of early Priestly writers during or shortly after the Exile. They present a visionary program, never fully realized, of the post-exilic restoration of the temple cult.

between blood and atonement: Gen 9:4; Deut 12:23; Lev 17:11, 14. The most complete of these is Lev 17:11.

> For the *life* of the flesh is in the blood; and I have given it for you upon the altar to make atonement for your *souls*; for it is the blood that makes atonement, by reason of the *life*.

The Hebrew word for life *nepeš* (italicized above) signifies *soul, living being, life, self, person, desire, appetite, emotion, passion.* The phrase "for your *souls*" really signifies "for you" or "for your persons." The other uses of *nepeš* in Lev 17:11 signify simply "life" or "seat of life." It definitely does *not* mean what we ordinarily think of as soul (Greek: *psychē*; Latin: *anima*), that is, something distinct from and separate from the body.

Lev 17:11 first explains why eating blood is prohibited: the life of the flesh is in the blood (and only the Lord has dominion over life). It then mentions the one use to which blood may be put: to make atonement with it upon the altar. It then explains that the blood does this because of the *nepeš* contained in it. Lev 17:11 in itself and in its context points to just one meaning: *The blood of the sacrificial animal atones by means of and by power of the life (nepeš) contained in this sacrificial animal.*[18]

Note well that the Hebrew of Lev 17:11 simply does *not* speak of substitution, despite the predilection of many translators for this idea. (The Catholic Confraternity accurately translates the verse in a nonsubstitutionary way, but then does open violence to the text by insisting in a footnote that the life of the animal victim substitutes for the life of the person offering!) This idea of substitution has dominated Christian sacrificial soteriology. There are overtones of it in the New Testament itself; it influenced many of the Fathers," and it is assumed in the Anselmian idea of penal satisfaction. Where, then, did it come from?

The idea of substitution is present in the Old Testament at least in the general sense that the rites of atonement "take the place of" or "substitute for" the necessity of suffering the con-

18. Cf. A. Metzinger, "Die Substitutionstheorie und das alttestamentliche Opfer mit besonderer Berücksichtigung von Lev. 17,11," *Bib* 21 (1940) 271–72.

sequences of one's transgressions.[19] Substitutionary elements are also present in other aspects of Israel's salvation-history.

Passover

The laws about redeeming or consecrating the firstborn and the first fruits are usually found in a Passover context. The blood of the original Passover lambs in Exodus 12 was the sign which saved Israel's firstborn. This inevitably aroused ideas of substitution in association with the Passover. Nevertheless, there is no evidence that the Old Testament considered the sacrifice of the Passover lamb to be an atoning death in the sense of vicarious penal suffering for, as we cannot repeat too often, it shows absolutely no interest in the death as such or in the suffering, if any, of the sacrificial animal.[20]

Vicarious Intercession of a Mediator[21]

This idea is present when the people intercede for Jonathan (1 Sam 14:45) and Abraham for Sodom (Gen 18:22–23), when Moses places himself between the people and God's chastising wrath (Exod 32:30–32), and in a similar prayer of David for the people (2 Sam 24:17). Thus the idea of vicarious atonement also seems to be present.

Vicarious Suffering and Death[22]

Apparently in response to the enigma of guiltless suffering, the idea of the just man atoning vicariously for Israel became common in early rabbinic Judaism, especially in relation to Moses and Isaac. By the third century A.D., whatever soteriological significance the Christians claimed for Jesus, the Jews in turn tended to claim for Moses or Isaac. But pre-Christian Judaism was apparently unfamiliar with the idea of a suffering, atoning

19. Cf. Eichrodt, Theology, 1. 165–67.

20. Cf. esp. N. Füglister, Die Heilsbedeutung des Pascha (SANT 8; Munich: Köscl, 1963) 68–71.

21. Cf. Eichrodt, Theology, 2. 448–52.
E. Lohse, Märtyrer und Gottesknecht (FRLANT 64; 2d ed.; Göttingen: Vandenhoeck & Ruprecht, 1963) 64–110.

22. Lohse, Märtyrer, 87–92; 105–7.

Messiah. Except possibly for Wis 2:13 and 3:1–9, the Fourth Servant Song (Isa 52:13–53:12) was not interpreted this way in early rabbinic Judaism.

Martyrdom

Both 2 Maccabees (first century B.C.) and 4 Maccabees (first century A.D.) contain a martyr theology which provides the most significant pre-Christian source for the idea of the vicarious, even atoning suffering and death of the martyrs. These ideas are strongly suggested in 2 Maccabees, especially 7:37–38 and 12:42–45, and they are articulated with clarity in 4 Maccabees, especially in the prayers of the dying martyrs. Eleazar prays the Lord to be "merciful unto thy people, and let our punishment be a satisfaction in their behalf. Make my blood their purification and take my soul to ransom their souls" (4 Macc 6:28–29).

Clearly then, the idea of substitution is present and increasingly strong as we near the end of the Old Testament period. But the idea that the whole sacrificial system of atonement was based on the idea of an animal's death substituting for that of a person no longer claims significant exegetical support, for it wanders far beyond the limits of the evidence, especially if one is thinking of penal substitution.

The idea of penal substitution, however, obviously did not materialize out of nothing. Apart from the growing interest in substitutionary ideas we have just documented from the Old Testament itself, the most influential single boost to substitutionary ideas was given by the Alexandrian Septuagint (LXX) translation of Lev 17:11 from the third century B.C. In a way that still puzzles commentators, the final phrase of this verse "It is the blood that makes atonement *by reason of the life*" (*b*e*nepeš* —instrumental beth) is translated into the Greek *anti tēs psychēs* which normally would mean *instead* (in place) *of the soul* (life). In fact, the LXX of Leviticus elsewhere translates the talic law (life for a life—*nepeš tahat nepeš*) precisely with this Greek construction. This translation—the form in which most New Testament and early Christians knew the Bible—suggests by itself that the life of the sacrificial animal makes atonement in place of the life of the offerer. However, not only is this meaning not supported by the Hebrew; it also creates serious theological problems such as the suggestion that God is a wrathful, punishing, jealous, avenging being.

The LXX, as a translation, is also an interpretation made with a particular view to its relevance for second and third century B.C. Greek-speaking Jews. Religiously, however, these translators were very conservative; for them consciously to add the notion of substitution where it did not already exist would have been unthinkable. It would, in fact, be the only instance of so radical a change in their entire translation. Metzinger ("Substitutionstheorie," 358–64) suggests that the translator(s), in a moment of perplexity, fell into this translation and may even have been quite happy to have stumbled onto a Greek translation which was more open than the Hebrew to the increasingly popular substitutionary ideas of his day. Moraldi, on the other hand, suggests that the LXX consciously chose *anti tēs psychēs* precisely in order to avoid suggesting the idea of substitution.[23]

No matter what might be the ultimate explanation, however, those who had no familiarity with the Hebrew Bible (i.e., almost all early Christians) would find the LXX of Lev 17:11 strongly evocative of substitutionary, even penal substitutionary ideas. This puzzling translation, strongly suggesting a meaning which the Hebrew original did not have, became a primary source for those exaggerated theories of penal substitution which many Christians have erroneously thought to be expressive of the central teaching of Christian sacrificial soteriology.

23. L. Moraldi, *Espiazione sacrificale e rite espiatori nell'ambiente biblico e nell'Antico Testamento* (AnBib 5; Rome: Pontifical Biblical Institute 1956) 241–43.

CHAPTER THREE

FROM THE OLD TESTAMENT
TO THE NEW

We now focus our attention on the time of Christianity's birth
out of Judaism. We will do so by treating successively a group
of themes, many of which have roots deep in history, but all of
which, near the end of the Old Testament period, underwent
developments which became significant in the rise of the Christian theology of sacrifice. After some remarks about the Greek
Septuagint (LXX) translation of the Old Testament, we will
take up the covenant sacrifice, Passover, circumcision, Qumran,
and the Akedah (sacrifice of Isaac).

THE SEPTUAGINT[1]

The Septuagint ("Seventy," hence LXX), the translation of the
Old Testament into Greek by Alexandrian Jews of the third and
second centuries B.C.E., was the Bible known by the early Christians. It established the religious and cultic language and terminology used by the New Testament writers. It was not a
translation of dead history but the communication of a living reality according to the same principles of living interpretation—"existential" we now call it—which governed the exegesis of the rabbis,
Philo, the sectarians at Qumran, and the New Testament itself.
Primitive anthropomorphisms are changed: for example, "hand"

1. See CS, 139–44. The most recent handbook on the Septuagint is that
of S. Jellicoe, *The Septuagint and Modern Study* (Oxford: Clarendon,
1968). The only work found to be very helpful for the theme of this book
is S. Daniel, *Recherches sur le vocabulaire du culte dans la Septante*
(Etudes et Commentaires 61; Paris: C. Klincksieck, 1966).

of God becomes "power." The translation is often the sign (perhaps also a cause) of significant changes in religious thinking, as when *ḥesed* ("lovingkindness") becomes *eleos* ("mercy" or "pity"), and *ṣedeq* ("righteous" or "righteousness") becomes *dikaiosynē* ("justice."). The most significant change in the areas of sacrifice is the troubling one discussed at the end of the previous chapter. The Hebrew expression "by means of the life" of the animals as translated into Greek means "in place of the life" of the person offering. Another but this time felicitous contribution is the translation *osmē euōdias*—"pleasing fragrance"—without the normal definite article. This suggests, as explained above, that God's acceptance of a sacrifice is not an objective, quantifiable reality controllable by us.

To sum up: the LXX formed the language of the New Testament and early Christian theology of sacrifice in three ways: 1) It translated some words into normal Greek equivalents found in pagan cultic practice. 2) More often it invented neologisms slightly different from normal Greek (a changed vowel or ending) calculated to emphasize that the reality spoken of is different from pagan counterparts. 3) In a few cases it simply transliterated from the Hebrew.

COVENANT SACRIFICE[2]

As we can see from the divine covenants with Noah (Gen 8:20–9:17) and Abraham (Gen 15), the act of making or "cutting" a covenant was a sacrificial ceremony. This is especially true of the Mosaic covenant sacrifice in Exod 24:3–8(E) which, together with the Passover and sacrifice of Isaac, is seen as one of the three foundational sacrificial events in the Old Testament. There, in a totally unique ceremony, Moses, acting as a priest,[3]

2. See *CS*, 89–93. Beyond the generally excellent articles dealing with covenant in the dictionaries and encyclopedias, and the works on the history and development of Old Testament sacrifice mentioned above in Chap. Two, R. Schmid, *Das Bundesopfer in Israel: Wesen, Ursprung und Bedeutung des alttestamentlichen Schelamim* (SANT 9; Munich: Kösel, 1964), proves most helpful.

3. Cf. H. H. Rowley, *Worship in Ancient Israel: Its Forms and Meaning* (Philadelphia: Fortress, 1967; London: SPCK, 1967) 52.

throws half the sacrificial blood against the altar and the other half upon the people as they ratify aloud the covenant which the Lord has just made with them.

Covenant sacrifice, however, did not get handed on in the sacrificial code (Lev 1–7) as a particular type of sacrifice like the burnt offering or sin offering, except as part of the "sacrifice of peace offerings" in Leviticus 3. The blood rite there encountered, *throwing* the blood against the altar (Lev 3:2, 8, 13), is the same as for the burnt offering (Lev 1:5, 11) but quite different from the *smearing, anointing,* and *sprinkling* rites of the sin offering (Lev 4:5–7). Apparently there was at one time a ceremony called the covenant or peace sacrifice (see Lev 7:14); when it fell into disuse its blood rite of the throwing type, together with its strong covenantal associations, had already become part of the burnt offering ritual.

In relation to the New Testament, one must recall that early rabbinic attitudes toward sacrifice failed increasingly to distinguish between the technicalities and the ideas associated with particular sacrificial rites. Ideas associated with the blood rite of the covenant sacrifice tended to become associated with the blood rites of any sacrifice, especially where the blood was tossed or thrown. For example, the author of Hebrews 9 (see below, p. 71), with little concern for original context, combined, for his own theological purposes, images, ideas, and rites from the Day of Atonement (Lev 16), the Exod 24:3–8 covenant sacrifice, the rites of sprinkling with the waters of purification (Num 19), and the vicarious atonement of the Suffering Servant (Isa 53).

THE PASSOVER[4]

The first Christians looked upon the Christ-event as a Passover event. This was so much taken for granted that the most concentrated witness to it is, in the context of Paul's letter, almost a

4. See *CS*, 121, 196–207. The most helpful single major work is N. Füglister, *Die Heilsbedeutung des Pascha* (SANT 8; Munich: Kösel, 1963) esp. 202–32. The essence of this work is accessible in English in distilled form as "Passover" in *Sacramentum Mundi* (New York: Herder, 1969) 4. 352–57.

throwaway line: "Christ, our paschal lamb, has been sacrificed" (1 Cor 5:7). The fact that the Passover was a sacrifice is seldom contested. It has a fascinating history in the Old Testament. It begins with the Egyptian Passover of Exodus 12 celebrated as a family feast. It then becomes the temple Passover of Deuteronomy 16 where it is joined with the Feast of Unleavened Bread and also turned into a great pilgrimage feast. It finally becomes the Jewish Passover, common in the time of Christ, which began with the lamb being slaughtered by priests in the temple and with an elaborate blood rite of *tossing* or *throwing* the blood at the altar with the strong covenantal associations already noted. One suspects that the compiler of the Mishnah tractate Pesahim considered this sacrificial blood rite to be the most essential part of the Passover observance.[5]

All four Gospels place the Lord's Supper in the context of the Passover feast in which three dimensions are operative: the past, the present, and the future.

The *past* is operative because Israel consistently historicized the Passover celebration into a memorial of the Exodus. The sentiments of Deut 16:1–6 and Exod 13:8 are expanded in the Mishnah which reflects attitudes current in Jesus' time:

> In every generation a man must so regard himself as if he came forth himself from out of Egypt, for it is written, And thou shalt tell thy son in that day saying, It is because of that which the Lord did for me when I came forth out of Egypt. Therefore we are bound to give thanks, to praise, to glorify, to honor, to exalt, to extol, and to bless him who wrought all these wonders for our fathers and for us. He brought us out from bondage and from darkness to great light, and from servitude to redemption. *Pesah.* 10:5 (Danby, *Mishnah*, 151)

And since early rabbinic Judaism tended to consider every significant salvation-history event as a Paschal event, the individual Jew regarded participation in this feast as a personal entry into the course of salvation-history.

The *present* is operative because the participants also believed

---

5. Cf. *Pesah.* 5:1–7; 8:3 in H. Danby, *The Mishnah* (Oxford: University Press, 1933) 141–42, 147.

themselves to be part of a salvific action here and now. This is due to the character of Passover as memorial and as sacrifice—as memorial, because both Israel and Yahweh recalled their parts in a real, objectively effective saving action; as sacrifice, because a real atoning effect was associated with most sacrifices by the time of Christ (especially those involving a lamb, as was usually the case with the Passover). We read in the late second century B.C. Book of Jubilees:

> And do thou command the children of Israel to observe the pass-over throughout their days, every year, once a year on the day of its fixed time, and it shall come for a memorial well pleasing before the Lord, and no plague shall come upon them to slay or to smite in that year in which they celebrate the passover in its season in every respect according to His command. (*Jub.* 49:15)[6]

The *future* is operative because Israel saw the original Passover as the archetype of the eschatological salvation event to come at the last day (cf. Isa 31:5; Hos 2:16; Jer 23:7; 31:31–32; Isa 40–45). The Passover celebration could be regarded as the occasion or anticipation of this final salvation event (cf. Isa 25:5; 30:29 with 2 Chr 30:21–27; 35:1–19), which was then itself to be seen as a Passover event. Finally, both Josephus and the Gospels show that the Passover was a time of intense messianic-eschatological expectation.[7]

The lamb was, almost without exception, the preferred sacrificial animal. The specific prescriptions for the Paschal lamb, a one-year-old male without blemish, are like those for the morning and evening daily burnt offering; in fact they are so similar that the rabbis make direct comparisons with the Passover sacrifice. Further, although the Old Testament nowhere prescribes a first-born animal for the Passover, all its regulations regarding the dedication/redemption of the firstborn are actually found in a Passover context. This has the effect of bringing together ideas of redemption and ransom with those of vicarious atonement (but not vicarious punishment or penal satisfaction, ideas quite foreign

6. R. H. Charles, *The Apocrypha and Pseudepigrapha of the Old Testament in English. Pseudepigrapha* (Oxford: Clarendon, 1913) 2. 80–81.

7. Josephus, *The War of the Jews* 2:3:1; 4:7:2; 5:3:11; *Antiquities* 17:9:3; 20:5:3; Luke 13:1; Mark 11:10 par; John 12:12–19.

to the Old Testament, as we have already emphasized). The Passover context of these themes implicitly provides for the Christian mind the background of the New Testament idea of Christ's vicarious ("for us") sacrificial death. It also helps explain the special preference and love for the firstborn/first fruits (cf. Wis 18:12–13; Gen 22:2) as the best material for sacrifice and as the most effective means and mediators of blessings. This idea was given extensive metaphorical use by Paul (Rom 8:23; 16:5 1 Cor 15:20, 23; 16:15; 2 Thess 2:13). It is also found in Jas 1:18 and Rev 14:4, and was later enthusiastically adopted by the Fathers. It is still alive today in such things as the special value pious Catholics put on a new priest's first Mass and first blessing.

In the New Testament itself the evangelists, especially John, took explicit pains to highlight Christ's death as the Christian Passover sacrifice.[8] The task was not too difficult, for the Mishnah *Pesah.* 7:1 instructions for roasting the Passover lamb put the animal into the shape of a cross, as Justin's Dialogue with Trypho 40:3 reminds us. The piercing of Christ's side (John 19:34) reminds one of Mishnah *Tamîd* 4:2. John 19:14 places the crucifixion precisely at the time for slaughtering the Passover lambs in the temple. The disappearance of the sun (Mark 15:33; Matt 27:45; Luke 23:44–45) probably alludes to the targumic interpretation of "between the two evenings" as the time for killing the Passover lamb. John's replacement of the Synoptics' *kalamos* (reed) to raise the sponge to Jesus' lips with hyssop (far too pliable for this purpose) seems explicable only as a conscious allusion to the hyssop in the blood rite of the Egyptian Passover (Exod 12:22). Finally, John 19:36 applies to Christ the regulation for preparing the Passover lamb: "Not a bone of him shall be broken."

THE BLOOD OF CIRCUMCISION[9]

Although the early history and meaning of circumcision which lay behind such texts as Genesis 34 and Exod 4:24–26 are obscure,

8. See especially Füglister, *Heilsbedeutung*, 63.

9. See *CS*, 187–95. Apart from the general background works already alluded to, see especially G. Vermes, "Baptism and Jewish Exegesis: New

it is clear that in later times this initiation rite (which is, itself, not a sacrifice) had become, together with the sabbath observance, one of the two principal signs of the covenant in post-exilic Judaism. There also grew up a line of interpretation which expressed a strong sacrificial or atoning significance in circumcision, especially through the close association of Passover blood and the blood of circumcision as developed in the *Palestinian Targums*.[10]

The words of Moses' wife Zipporah in Exod 4:25: "You are a bridegroom of blood to me," become in the Septuagint: "Behold the blood of the circumcision of my child." This suggests that Moses was delivered from death by the (sacrificial) expiatory power of the blood of circumcision, an interpretation supported by the *Palestinian Targums*: on Exod 4:25, "Now may the blood of this circumcision atone for the guilt of my husband"; on Exod 4:26, "How beloved is the blood of [this] circumcision which has saved my husband from the hand of the Angel of Death [Destroying Angel]." This interpretation can be dated as early as the second century B.C.

A strong tendency to associate circumcision with Passover is verifiable both in the Old Testament (cf. Exod 4:24–26; Josh 5:2–9; Exod 12:43–45, 48) and especially in the haggadah (nonlegal devotional literature) which enthusiastically develops the "legend of the two bloods," that is, that the blood of circumcision was mingled with the blood of the first Passover lambs. For example, *Targum Pseudo-Jonathan* on Exod 12:13: "You shall mix the blood of the Passover sacrifice and of circumcision and make of it a sign to put on the houses where you live; I will see the merit of the blood and will spare you." Among numerous other references to this theme, the most interesting one seems to be a passage from the *Targum on the Canticle of Canticles* (which was read at Passover time):

Light from Ancient Sources," *NTS* 4 (1958) 309–19 (republished in revised form as "Circumcision and Exodus IV 24–26" in *Scripture and Tradition in Judaism* (SPB 4; Leiden: Brill, 1961) 178–92; for the spiritualization of the concept: H.-J. Hermission, *Sprache und Ritus im altisraelitischen Kult: Zur "Spiritualisierung" der Kultbegriffe im Alten Testament* (WMANT 19; Neukirchen-Vluyn: Neukirchener Verlag, 1965) 64–76.

10. The Targums are Aramaic interpretative translations of the Scriptures which were used in Jewish community (synagogue) worship.

At the time when the glory of Yahweh was manifested in Egypt on the night of the Passover in order to kill the first-born . . . he protected the houses where we were, lay in wait by the window, watched by the trellis, and saw the blood of the Passover sacrifice and the blood of the circumcision stamped on our doors. . . . He looked down from the height of the heavens and saw the people eating the sacrifice of the feast and he spared them and he did not give power to the Destroying Angel to destroy us.[11]

The Hebrew text of Ezek 16:6 has an apparently nonsensical repetition of the phrase: "I said to you in your bloods, live." Most translations, including the Septuagint, simply omit the repetition; but the Targums make a virtue of this repetition by referring it to the legend of the two bloods:

Because the memorial of the covenant with your fathers is before Me, I revealed Myself to deliver you, for it is known before Me that you are oppressed in your captivity. I said to you: Because of the blood of the circumcision I will take care of you. I said to you again: Because of the blood of the Passover I will redeem you.[12]

The theological significance of the blood of circumcision is considerable, for it is drawn inexorably into the same sphere of ideas we have already seen to be associated with sacrifice and atonement in general, and Passover and covenant in particular. We are not surprised, then, to find the rabbis insisting, for the validity of circumcision, that at least one drop of blood must flow. This seems, by association, to be an illustration of the rabbinic principle which even the New Testament quotes: "Without the shedding of blood there is no forgiveness of sins" (Heb 9:22). This theological development probably took place before the idea of law-observance had become dominant in Jewish soteriology in the second century B.C. (see above, p. 24).

Much of the Pauline and deutero-Pauline theology of baptism, not merely as initiation and purification but above all as a participation in the sacrificial death and resurrection of Christ, as a

11. As quoted by R. Le Déaut, *La Nuit Pascale: Essai sur la signification de la Pâque juive à partir du Targum d'Exode XII. 42* (AnBib 22; Rome: Pontifical Biblical Institute, 1963) 211.

12. As quoted in Vermes, "Circumcision and Exodus IV 24–26," 191.

"circumcision of Christ" (Col 2:11), seems indebted to this background. A careful reading of Rom 6:3-4 and Col 2:11-12 with this in mind is illuminating. But Paul's radical christologizing of the idea of circumcision not only tends to spiritualize it metaphorically, but also, at times, to dispense with its basic Jewish meaning: "In Christ Jesus neither circumcision nor uncircumcision is of any avail, but faith through love" (Gal 5:6); "For we are the true circumcision, who worship God in spirit, and glory in Christ Jesus, who put no confidence in the flesh" (Phil 3:3).

QUMRAN: THE COMMUNITY AS TEMPLE

The Dead Sea Scrolls (see CS, 157-74) are a fairly extensive body of manuscripts and fragments discovered in the years following 1947 in some dozen caves to the west of the Dead Sea. They apparently represent the library of the Jewish sect centered at the recently excavated Qumran site. These writings, all stemming from the time prior to the Jewish-Roman War of A.D. 66-70, contain the single most important nonbiblical source for the background of the early Christian idea of sacrifice.

The Qumran texts contain a consistent temple symbolism, in which the community is represented as the new temple, and in which the true sacrifice is seen as being spiritual in character, offered in the holy and pure lives, the praise and the prayer of the members of the community. No direct parallel to this temple symbolism has been traced in Judaism.[13]

13. B. Gärtner, *The Temple and Community in Qumran and the New Testament: A Comparative Study in the Temple Symbolism of the Qumran Texts and the New Testament* (SNTSMS 1; Cambridge: University Press, 1965) 47. Other studies helpful on the place of sacrifice in Qumran are: J. M. Baumgarten, "Sacrifice and Worship among the Jewish Sectarians of the Dead Sea (Qumran) Scrolls," *HTR* 46 (1953) 141-59 J. Carmignac, "L'utilité ou l'inutilité des sacrifices sanglants dans la 'Règle de la Communauté' de Qumran," *RB* 63 (1956) 524-32; H. Ringgren, *The Faith of Qumran: Theology of the Dead Sea Scrolls*, trans. E. T. Sander (Philadelphia: Fortress, 1963) esp. 201-54. For a summary of the theme "community as temple" see R. J. McKelvey, *The New Temple: The Church in the New Testament* (Oxford Theological Monographs; Oxford: University Press, 1969) 46-53.

The development of this temple symbolism was stimulated by the particular religious situation of the Qumran sectarians. They were, of all the Jews, probably the most intensely aware of God's transcendent holiness and their desperate need for atonement. But the process of atonement was still centered in ritual sacrifice which could be offered only in the Jerusalem temple, a temple whose cult they believed to be invalid because of tampering with the sacred calendar and with the membership rolls of the priesthood. This intolerable situation forced them to find surrogates for the sacrificial rites of atonement, while eagerly awaiting, as the *War Scroll* shows (1QM 2:1-6), the full restoration of the true cult.

The Qumran *Community Rule* or *Manual of Discipline* (1QS) from Qumran Cave 1 is our major source. In the third column of that scroll (1QS 3:6-12) the word *kipper* (signifying sacrificial atonement) is used three times in reference not to sacrifices but to nonsacrificial rites and actions which the Qumran sectarians considered as having an atoning effect; and at the end of the passage, the emphasis is not on the rite but on the internal dispositions of the worshiper. In the fifth column of this scroll we find a rather clearly spiritualized use of the concept of circumcision signifying a *community asceticism* whose purpose is to *make atonement* for the members of the community (1QS 5:4-7). This at least implies that the community was taking over the function of the temple as the place where atonement takes place.

The clearest expression of the Qumran community-temple theology is in the eighth column of the *Manual of Discipline*:

It [the Council of the Community] shall be an everlasting Plantation, a House of Holiness for Israel, an Assembly of the *Holy of Holies* for Aaron. They shall be witnesses to the truth at the Judgment, and shall be the elect of Goodwill who shall *atone for* the Land and pay to the wicked their reward. It shall be that tried wall, that precious cornerstone, whose foundations shall neither rock nor sway in their place (Isa 28:16). It shall be a *Holy of Holies* for Aaron, with everlasting knowledge of the covenant of justice, and shall offer up sweet fragrance (*rêaḥ niḥoaḥ*). It shall be a House of Perfection and Truth in Israel that they may establish a Covenant according to the everlasting precepts. And they shall be an agreeable offering, *atoning for the land.* (1QS 8:5–10)[14]

Here the *Council of the Community* (not priests offering sacrifice) has become the agent of atonement, specifically by means of "the practice of justice" and "suffering the sorrows of affliction." Then, after applying its own type of existential reinterpretation to the foundation-cornerstone image of Isa 28:16, the passage moves on to make the startling identification of the *Council of the Community* with the *Most Holy Place* of the temple. This is the *debir,* the innermost sanctuary where Yahweh is present, the place entered but once a year by the high priest, enveloped in protective clouds of incense, to make atonement for the temple, the land, and the people. The community thus not only sees itself as performing the atoning functions of the temple, but also *sees itself as the very sacrifice* offered in this spiritual temple. Column 9 of the *Manual of Discipline* then makes it clear that it was not just the Council of the Community but indeed the whole community which was looked on as the atoning temple:

When these (the ordinary members of the sect) become members of the Community in Israel according to all these rules, they shall establish the spirit of holiness according to everlasting truth. They shall atone for guilty rebellion and for sins of unfaithfulness that they may obtain lovingkindness for the land more than from the flesh of burnt offerings and the fat of sacrifice. And an offering of the lips rightly offered shall be an acceptable fragrance of righteousness and perfection of way as a delectable free-will offering. (1QS 9:3–5)

A Cave 4 text, apparently representing a later stage of Qumran thought, makes this temple spiritualization even more explicit.

And he proposed to build him a Sanctuary of men (or, among men) in which should be offered sacrifices before him, the works of the Law. (4QFlor 1:6–7)

Only Christology separates these passages from a New Testa-

14. The translation of the Scrolls we use is that of G. Vermes, *The Dead Sea Scrolls in English* (2d ed.; Harmondsworth/Baltimore: Penguin Books, 1965).

ment passage such as 1 Pet 2:4–10 where Christians are described as living stones being built up into the holy temple, in which spiritual sacrifices are offered to God, and of which Christ is the cornerstone. Quite probably, then, we have a thematic relationship between Qumran and the New Testament idea of the community (and individual) as the new and true temple (esp. 2 Cor 6:16 and 1 Pet 2:5). There is also, in the idea of an angelic or heavenly liturgy, a significant relationship of contrast. Whereas the Qumran sectarians thought of themselves as sharing here and now in a liturgy with angels whose presence and mediating power were of enormous soteriological significance for them, the Christians not only situated the heavenly liturgy in heaven, but also reserved mediating power to the one mediator Jesus Christ.

THE AKEDAH (SACRIFICE OF ISAAC)[15]

Even more than the Passover and the covenant sacrifice, the Akedah (i.e., "binding"—Gen 22:9) of Isaac is in many ways the great "founding" sacrifice of the Old Testament. Its historical origins are at best conjectural, for we know of it only through the Elohist who, some eight centuries after Abraham, clothed his narrative in the form of the burnt offering ritual of his own day (see above, pp. 14–16). In this Elohistic form, three theological themes stand out: 1) the rejection of human sacrifice, 2) the identification of the site (Mt. Moriah) with that of the Jerusalem temple, 3) the theological heart of the story: Abraham's faith-obedience relationship with God which elicits God's blessings upon him and his descendants. The haggadic development of the Akedah, to which we now turn, provides invaluable insights into the soteriology of early rabbinic Judaism, and actually supplies the single most important piece of background for the sacrificial soteriology of the New Testament.

15. CS, 175–86. The most recent full treatment is R. Daly, "The Soteriological Significance of the Sacrifice of Isaac," CBQ 39 (1977) 45–75. In a growing body of literature, particularly noteworthy are: G. Vermes, "Redemption and Genesis XXII" in Scripture and Tradition in Judaism (SPB 4; Leiden: Brill, 1964) 193–227, and Le Déaut, La Nuit Pascale, 131–212.

The *Palestinian Targums*,[16] especially in the "Poem of the Four Nights," a commentary on Exod 12:42, are the richest single source for the Akedah.[17] It encompasses salvation-history in the four "nights" of creation, of Abraham's covenant (Gen 15) and sacrificing of Isaac (Gen 22), of the Passover, and of the end of the world. The major theological developments, that is, beyond the Genesis 22 narrative, are the following: (a) the Akedah is viewed as the actual source of the Passover's efficacy; (b) Isaac is portrayed as a thirty-seven-year-old man voluntarily acquiescing in the sacrifice; (c) Isaac is spoken of as actually having been sacrificed, which explains why the haggadah speaks of the "ashes" or "blood" of Isaac, one version calling him "the lamb of the burnt offering"; (d) Isaac, but not Abraham, experiences a vision; (e) Abraham prays that his obedience and Isaac's covenant will be *remembered* by God for the benefit of their descendants. Two versions give this prayer an explicitly expiatory form.[17]

The antiquity and substance of this Akedah theology are both confirmed and amplified in a rich variety of Jewish literature from the last century B.C. and first century A.D. The Book of Jubilees 17:15–18:19 specifies the site as Mount Zion, dates the event at the Passover, and treats the Passover explicitly as a commemoration of the Akedah. Philo, especially in de Abrahamo 167–207, portrays Abraham and Isaac as lofty Stoic heroes in complete harmony of will as they actually carry out the sacrifice. In Philo theological attention is focused on the act of obedience of Abraham who functions as a priest in returning to God the gift of his son. The deliverance is God's returning the gift. In 4 Maccabees, 6:17–21; 7:11–14; 13:12; 16:18–20; 17:20–22 emphasize the Stoic quality of Abraham and Isaac's conduct and portray them as models for the Jewish martyrs whose atoning power is implicitly derived from that of the Akedah. Josephus in *Antiquities* I, 13, 222–36 stresses both the obedient piety and meritorious achievement of the two heroes and the joyous consent of Isaac,

16. The *Palestinian Targum* in the material that concerns us here is extant in four quite similar versions which date back almost to the time of Christ.

17. Other places in the Targums which mention the Akedah are: *Tg.* Lev 22:27; *Tg.* Cant 1:13; 2:17; 3:6; *Tg.* Esth 2. 5:1; *Tg.* 1 Chr 21:15.

the mature man. He also bathes the event in a liturgical atmosphere, like Philo, portraying it as the returning of a gift to God. The culmination of this development is found in Pseudo-Philo's *Bib. Ant.* 18:5; 23:8; 32:1–4; 40:2–4. Isaac is conscious of being the type of sacrifice God desires; its unique position in relation to all other sacrifices is stressed; God accepts the sacrifice as a memorial and in expiation for future generations; and finally, great emphasis is placed on the idea that the merit of the Akedah (and of any sacrifice) depends on the internal dispositions of the offerer.

By New Testament times the haggadah on the Akedah contained a fairly well-developed soteriology. First, Isaac's self-oblation was regarded as a true sacrifice in its own right. References to the "ashes" of Isaac (*Tg.* 1 Chr 21:15) and to the atoning force of his "blood" (*Bib. Ant.* 18:6) indicate that references to the actual sacrificing of Isaac were at times more than a mere mental construct. The unique feature of this sacrifice (thus overcoming the great internal weakness of Old Testament sacrifice as an act of religion) was the free consent of the victim, the righteous ancestor of the Chosen People. Thus one tended in turn to look upon his sacrifice as the sacrifice par excellence. Second, the effects of the Akedah were believed to be redemptive. This is indicated not only by the clear statements to this effect but also by the close association of the Akedah with the great moments of deliverance and blessing in Israel's history. Third, even more specifically, the Akedah had a special causal relationship to the atoning efficacy of all other sacrifices. This is explicitly stated in Leviticus Rabbah on Lev 5:1, 10 and by three of the four versions of the *Palestinian Targum* on Lev 22:27. Finally, the liturgical "situation-in-life" of the Akedah haggadah is the Passover feast. The bond between these two great events is a doctrinal one, that is, "The saving virtue of the Passover lamb proceeded from the merits of that first lamb, the son of Abraham, who offered himself upon the altar."[18] So many of the sources of this haggadah are of such verifiable antiquity that we can confidently accept it as a reliable sketch of Jewish sacrificial soteri-

18. Vermes, "Redemption and Genesis XXII," 215.

ology at the time the New Testament was being written. The very large amount of this material contained in the *Palestinian Targum* enables us also to assume confidently that it was familiar to those early Christians who had converted from Judaism.

That the Akedah does not play a more obvious role than it does in New Testament soteriology is something of a puzzle. Perhaps it was largely taken for granted. But perhaps also the early Christians were a bit reserved in the use of something which was obviously very "Jewish." New Testament allusions to the Akedah are, nonetheless, significant.

Certain References to the Akedah in the New Testament

Heb 11:17–20 speaks as if the sacrifice had actually occurred, then goes on to speak of God's power "to raise men even from the dead." Jas 2:21 also speaks of the sacrifice as accomplished. The faith-works theology of James also evokes the haggadic tendency to view the Akedah as the meritorious achievement *par excellence*. Rom 8:32 "He who did not spare his own son" evokes the Septuagint of Gen 22:16. The continuation of Rom 8:32 "but gave him up for us all" supports the allusion to the Akedah. Similar uses of "to give, to give up" in Gal 1:4; 2:20; Eph 5:2, 25; Tit 2:14; and 1 Tim 2:6 to express Christ's loving act of self-immolation also recall the targumic portrayal of Isaac's self-immolation.

Probable References

John 3:16 "God so loved the world that he gave his only Son, that whoever believes in him should not perish but have eternal life." Mark 1:11 and 9:7 and their synoptic parallels (the voice from heaven in the baptism and transfiguration stories): "Thou art my beloved son; with thee I am well pleased" almost certainly allude to the Septuagint wording of Gen 22:2 "Take your beloved son, the one you love. . . ." These two stories are also permeated with other Akedah motifs, notably that of theophany. This motif, one of the oldest elements of the baptism and transfiguration stories, is also at the very heart of the Akedah, as we can see in the targumic "Poem of the Four Nights":

The heavens were let down and descended and Isaac saw their
perfection. . . .
On the fourth night, . . . Moses shall come out of the wilderness
and the King of Messiah out of Rome.
The one shall be lead upon a cloud, and the Word of the Lord
shall lead between them and they shall go forward together.[19]

The thematic affinity with the baptism and transfiguration theophanies is unmistakable, but not such as to allow us to decide
the question of literary source or literary analogue. In respect to
1 Cor 15:4, "Raised on the third day in accordance with the
scriptures," countless exegetes have struggled to find where
previous Scripture might mention resurrection on the third day,
not realizing that this Scripture fulfillment refers not to "raised"
but to *on the third day.*" For "on the third day" (Gen 22:4)
Abraham came to the place for sacrificing Isaac. In Israel's salvation-history, the "third day" was a characteristic time (some
thirty instances in the Old Testament) of salvation achieved or
crisis averted. Since, in the religious consciousness of New Testament times, the Akedah was one of the most notable of these
"third day" events, an allusion to it in 1 Cor 15:4 seems implicit.[20]
Finally, Gal 3:14 "That in Christ Jesus the blessings of Abraham
might come upon the Gentiles" appears to be a paraphrase of
Gen 22:18.

Possible References

Possible New Testament references to the Akedah are numerous. Gal 1:4, 2:20; Eph 5:2, 25; Titus 2:14; 1 Tim 2:6, in their
use of the verb "to give" to express Christ's self-giving strongly
evoke the Akedah gift motif of Philo, Josephus, and Pseudo-
Philo. In Matt 12:18 and Mark 12:6 the Greek *agapētos* (beloved) seems to be influenced by the similar Septuagint translation of the Hebrew *yaḥîd* in Gen 22:2, 12, 16. The pre-election
of the sacrificial lamb, referred to in 1 Pet 1:19–20, is an Akedah

19. Vermes, "Redemption and Genesis XXII," 216.
20. Cf. K. Lehmann, *Auferweckt am dritten Tag nach der Schrift.
Früheste Christologie, Bekenntnisbildung und Schriftauslegung im Lichte
von 1 Kor. 15,3–5* (Quaestiones Disputatae 38; Freiburg/Vienna: Herder,
1968) 176–81; 262–90.

motif. John 1:29, "The lamb of God who takes away the sins of the world," recalls Abraham addressing Isaac as "the lamb of the burnt offering" in the *Neofiti Targum* to Gen 22:8. Finally, the eucharistic inaugurative command in 1 Cor 11:24–25 and Luke 22:19 reminds us how the Akedah portrays God as "remembering" the merits of Isaac's sacrifice at the moment of the daily offering of lambs, at specific critical moments in Israel's salvation-history, and at the moment of the first Passover in Egypt.

To sum up: the Genesis 22 account of the sacrifice of Isaac was so richly elaborated by the haggadah that by New Testament times the Akedah had developed into a full expression of Jewish sacrificial soteriology. The sacrifice to which the mature Isaac consented was looked upon as if actually consummated. It was God's remembering of the Akedah that caused him to deliver and bless Israel at the first Passover and at the other moments of deliverance and blessing in its history. More specifically, the sacrificial cult was thought to be effective because it reminded God of the Akedah, the sacrifice par excellence. Admittedly, we cannot advance much beyond probabilities in determining relationships to specific New Testament texts; the classifications given above must be seen as provisional. I would, nevertheless, submit that it is now proven not only that such relationships exist, but also that the sacrificial soteriology of the New Testament can no longer be adequately discussed apart from the Akedah.

CHAPTER FOUR

THE NEW TESTAMENT

INTRODUCTION AND METHOD[1]

The New Testament says surprisingly little about sacrifice, apparently because Christianity grew more from the nomistic line of Jewish religious thought (especially the Pharisaic traditions with their emphasis on the law) than from the cultic line (the priests and Sadducees with their emphasis on ritual observance). Exceptions to this are Revelation, which centers on worship in the heavenly Jerusalem, and Hebrews, the first major attempt to explain how the new covenant fulfills and supersedes the Old Testament sacrificial cult. But even apart from these writings the New Testament provides an ample foundation for a Christian theology of sacrifice.

Our best method of approach is not immediately obvious. Scholars generally agree on the chronology of the New Testament writings, but this alone would be inadequate for us. The Gospels, our almost exclusive source for the life and teaching of Jesus, are not among the earliest New Testament works. The Pauline epistles, which are the earliest New Testament writings, together with some later epistles dependent on Paul, are our richest sources for a New Testament theology of sacrifice. But they are dependent on the preaching which only later took the precise written form we know as the Gospels. Every approach thus

1. See *CS*, 208–307. As is shown in the appropriate pages of *Christian Sacrifice*, extensive research in the best available literature lies behind what is presented here. I will usually refer to this literature, however, only when it has been particularly significant in the development of important aspects of my own work.

involves some circularity which even the best exegesis cannot entirely eliminate. To some extent we can and must bypass the complexities of New Testament chronology and of the theological growth increasingly recoverable in the New Testament. For the early Christians who based their theology of sacrifice on the New Testament were themselves largely innocent of its complexities. This situation suggests the following order of treatment which combines a systematic with a chronological approach while continually drawing upon the best that contemporary exegesis can offer: the Synoptic Gospels, Acts, the Pauline and deutero-Pauline letters, Hebrews, the Johannine writings, Revelation.

THE SYNOPTIC GOSPELS[2]

In the *infancy narratives*, Matt 2:11 uses technical sacrificial terms to describe the gifts, especially frankincense, which the Magi offered. Zechariah's vision about the future birth of John the Baptist occurred as he was performing the morning incense offering in the temple (Luke 1:8–23).

From the *teaching and activity of Jesus*, some texts imply a favorable attitude toward sacrifice. Chief among these is Matt 5:23–24 where Jesus instructs us to leave our gift before the altar and first be reconciled with our brother before making our offering.[3] Jesus' instruction to the cured leper to offer the prescribed sacrifice seems to take the sacrificial system for granted (Mark 1:44 parr). Similarly, his praise of the poor widow's offering (Mark 12:41–44 par) and his sharp criticism of the abuse of "Corban" (Mark 7:9–13 parr) make sense only in the context of a basically positive attitude toward sacrifice.

Other texts about Jesus' teaching and activity imply criticism of sacrifice. His defense of the disciples' plucking grain on the

2. See *CS*, 209–25.

3. There are significant parallels to this teaching in Jewish literature, e.g., Mishnah *Yoma* 8:9 (H. Danby, *The Mishnah* [Oxford University, 1933] 172); Qumran CD 9:13. Cf. A. Büchler, *Studies in Sin and Atonement in the Rabbinic Literature of the First Century* (Library of Biblical Studies; New York: KTAV, 1967; original ed. 1928) 403–18 and elsewhere in the Synoptics: Mark 11:25 parr; Matt 9:13; 12:7; Mark 12:29–33.

sabbath (Matt 12:1–8 parr) clearly implies Jesus' superiority to
the temple, and thus helps prepare for a fundamental break on
the part of the Christians with the temple cult. Although the
Cleansing of the Temple (Mark 11:15–19 parr) of itself reflects
only zeal for the purity of the temple, Jesus' quote of Isa 56:7,
". . . house of prayer for all nations," both implies criticism and
gives a spiritualizing thrust; it recalls that Jesus seemed to use
the temple for prayer and preaching but not for offering sacrifice.
There are six different New Testament versions of the Mark 14:58
par logion: ". . . destroy this temple that is made with hands
(cheiropoiētos) . . . another not made with hands *(acheiropoiē-
tos)*." Whether originating in the accounts of Jesus' trial or of
the temple-cleansing, the word *cheiropoiētos* is used by the Greek
Septuagint exclusively to signify or refer to idolatry and false
worship. To Jewish ears its use in these passages constitutes a
blasphemy against God's house. The parable of the Good Samaritan (Luke 10:29–37) likewise implies a strong criticism of the
cult, for priests and Levites were expected to keep away from
any "defiling" thing (such as a dead body) which would tem-
porarily disqualify them from participation in public worship.
Mark 12:10 parr, with its quotation of Ps 118:22, "The very stone
which the builders rejected has become the head of the corner"
implies criticism of sacrifice, especially for one aware of how
Qumran (1QS 8:7–8; 1QH 6:26) and 1 Pet 2:4–10 use this psalm
to support the community-as-temple motif.

Mark 10:45 (Matt 20:28), "The Son of Man came not to be
served but to serve and to give his life as a ransom for many," is
one of the great sacrificial sayings of Jesus.[4] *"For many"* suggests
Isa 53:10–12, hence Servant-of-God, sacrifice, and martyrdom.
"To give his life" reminds one of similar expressions which are
also implicitly sacrificial in John 10:11, 15, 17; it evokes the same
meaning as the Pauline texts which speak of Christ's sacrificial
self-giving. It also reminds us that true Christian sacrifice re-
turns to God the gift which is nothing other than one's own self
joyfully and unreservedly put at God's disposition. In the end,

4. C. F. D. Moule, *The Sacrifice of Christ* (Facet Books, Biblical
Series 12; Philadelphia: Fortress, 1964) 11.

however, we can do justice to this text only by interpreting it, as does Luke 22:24–27, in conjunction with the Servant themes of the eucharistic institution.

Thus, some sayings of Jesus imply approval, but the synoptic authors generally portray Jesus as critical of the sacrificial system. His coming has replaced the Old Testament cultic dispensation with a "liturgy" of love and service. This theme, however, far from being a radically new Christian invention, was already incipiently present in the Jewish religious thought of New Testament times.

Each of the four accounts of eucharistic institution (Matt 26:26–29; Mark 14:22–25; Luke 22:15–20; 1 Cor 11:23–25) formed from earliest times an integral part of the Passion Narrative. There was a basic identity between Jesus' last meal and his death. The Lord's Supper, as indicated by its numerous cultic terms and sacrificial allusions, was a revelation of Christ's saving action, a cultic anticipation or "prophecy in act" which pointed toward and explained the significance of Jesus' death.

Whether or not the historical Last Supper was an actual Passover meal, it was unquestionably thought of by the evangelists as a Passover event (Mark 14:12–27; Matt 26:17–20; Luke 22:7–14; John 13:1). Even the inaugurative command "Do this in memory of me" (Luke 22:19; 1 Cor 11:24–25) seems to allude to the remembrance aspects of the Passover.

"My blood of the [new] covenant" (Mark 14:24; Matt 26:28) recalls the Exod 24:3–8 covenant sacrifice. By adding "new" Luke and Paul bring in the famous "new covenant" passage of Jer 31:31–34. All the Synoptics have the sacrificially colored "poured out for many [you]," while Matt 26:28 makes explicit the atoning significance attached to almost all sacrifice at this time by adding: "for the forgiveness of sins." Thus the words of institution clearly look ahead to Jesus' death as bloody, sacrificial, and atoning.

At the most profound level, however, it is Servant Christology which dominates the primitive kerygma and also supplies the theological context of the words of institution. The phrases "shed for you [many]" and "given up for many" and Paul's "on

the night when he was betrayed" are both verbal and thematic
allusions to the Fourth Servant Song of Isaiah 53. The inaugurative command and the mention of the *new* covenant also seem
to allude to some of the other Servant Songs (Isa 49:1, 8; 42:6, 9).

The eucharistic "body" and "blood" find their fullest meaning
in this Servant of God framework. For it is misleading to see
these words as corresponding primarily to the Hebrew sacrificial
terms *flesh* and *blood*, thus presupposing the slaughtering which
separates these sacrificial elements.[5] This interpretation seems
not only to conflict with the Old Testament background which
never emphasized the death of the animal victim, but also to
subvert the intention of Jesus who repeatedly emphasized not the
aspect of himself as the victim but the free and voluntary character of his death as an act of self-giving. This aspect of Jesus'
death is greatly illumined when we give to "body" (Greek: *sōma*)
the sense it had in primitive apostolic language (cf. Rom 12:1),
that is, the *concrete living person*—in this case, the figure of Jesus
as the Servant of God in vicarious martyrdom reminiscent of
Isaiah 53. To sum up:

> It is not the idea of cultic sacrifice in which the body is seen as a
> separable part of the sacrifice, but rather that of a martyr's offer-
> ing which signifies the offering of one's body as the self-giving of
> one's whole person. Thus the sacrificial idea is also contained in
> the words over the bread; but this idea should not be seen in the
> understanding of the term *sōma* as isolated sacrificial flesh sep-
> arated from the blood; it must rather be looked for in the whole
> participial phrase and seen in its martyrological coloring.[6]

Thus "blood" is also to be read as signifying primarily the person
of Jesus, seen under the aspect of his suffering and dying.

5. As proposed by J. Jeremias, *The Eucharistic Words of Jesus*, trans N.
Perrin (rev. ed.; Philadelphia: Fortress, 1977) 221–25. This view seems
to overlook the fact that a whole meal originally intervened between the
two "consecrations." The words over the bread had to be able to stand
alone with full sacrificial meaning and could not depend on the words over
the cup for sense.

6. Translated from J. Betz, *Die Eucharistie in der Zeit der griechischen
Väter* (2d ed.; Freiburg/Vienna: Herder, 1964) II/1. 40–41. A summary in English of J. Betz's eucharistic theology can be found in "Eucharist, I. Theological" in *Sacramentum Mundi* (New York: Herder, 1968) 2.
257–67.

It is from this background that we can now more adequately speak of the Eucharist, or the historical Lord's Supper, as Christ's personal self-offering. As a cultic anticipation of Calvary, the Lord's Supper takes its meaning from Christ's death. But it cannot be emphasized too often, that death is the absolutely free, totally voluntary self-offering of Christ the Servant. The New Testament church seems to have clearly perceived this, for while, on the one hand, it used the Passover as the external framework for the Last Supper and Passion narratives, it used, on the other hand, Servant Christology to illuminate the inner significance of the Eucharist and the Passion.

All that we said above (pp. 49–52) about the Akedah (sacrifice of Isaac) in New Testament times is also relevant here. In fact, the parallels between the Akedah and Christ's sacrifice are striking, especially in the idea of the sacrifice of a human being characterized by perfect dispositions of willing self-offering on the part of the person sacrificed. Thus the most sublime ideas of perfect sacrifice and perfect dispositions for sacrifice found in the figure of the Suffering Servant, the Maccabean martyr-theology, and above all in the Akedah, find their most perfect expression and fulfillment in the New Testament doctrine of the sacrifice of Christ.

THE ACTS OF THE APOSTLES

The author of Acts (see CS, 225–31) was familiar with the christological Servant-theme, for he uses it when Philip the Deacon takes verses from the Fourth Servant Song (Isa 53:7–8) as an occasion to preach to the Ethiopian eunuch "the good news of Jesus" (Acts 8:26–40; cf. Luke 24:25–27, 48). But the sacrificial and atoning character of Jesus' death does not seem to be particularly emphasized by Luke.

The temple, however, does receive special attention.[7] As in the Synoptics, it is treated both positively and negatively. The new Christians pray there (2:46; 3:1–4:3; 21:26; 22:17); Peter and

7. See R. J. McKelvey, *The New Temple: The Church in the New Testament* (London: Oxford University Press, 1969) 84–91.

John perform a miracle there (3:1–3); and Paul was apparently praying there when, in a vision, he received his mission to the Gentiles—which, of course, suggests that the temple had seen its day. This is picked up in the fierce temple criticism of Stephen in chapters 6 and 7. In 7:41–50 Stephen calls the golden calf episode of Exod 32:4–6 a rejoicing "in the works of their hands," reinterprets Amos 5:25–27 to imply that idolatry is at the very root of Jewish sacrificial practice, then nails home his argument by proclaiming (by way of Isa 66:1) that the Most High does not dwell in houses "made with hands" (*cheiropoiētos*), that is, idolatrous human constructions (see above, p. 55). He calls the temple an idolatrous artifact. No wonder the Jews stoned him!

THE PAULINE THEOLOGY OF SACRIFICE

Passages from the principal Pauline letters complemented by others from 1 Peter and the deutero-Pauline letters contain the solid outline of a genuine theology of sacrifice (see *CS*, 230–56). Paul takes sacrifice for granted as part of the religious picture and obviously expects the Corinthians to follow his understanding of the Eucharist as a kind of communion sacrifice (1 Cor 10:14–22). He is basically Jewish in his attitudes except for the fundamental christocentricity of his thought, which also causes him to follow Jesus' lead in believing that the impure no longer necessarily contaminates the pure (see 1 Cor 7:14).

Paul's theology of sacrifice readily divides into three themes which also provide the basic outline for the early Christian theology of sacrifice: 1) the sacrifice of Christ, 2) the Christians as the new temple, 3) the sacrifice of (performed by) the Christians.

The Sacrifice of Christ

Paul is the earliest written Christian witness to this idea. His treatment of the Eucharist in 1 Corinthians 10 and 11 as a cultic anticipation of Christ's sacrificial death and as a participation in the blood and in the body of Christ, makes sense only on the supposition that he and his readers view the Lord's Supper and the Passion as sacrificial events. In the New Testament epistles this comes up repeatedly in the idea of Christ dying or giving himself up for us (2 Cor 5:14-15; Rom 5:6-11; 8:23; Gal 2:20; Eph 5:2, 25; Col 1:24; 1 Tim 2:5-6; Titus 2:13-14; 1 John 3:16). "Christ our paschal lamb has been sacrificed" (1 Cor 5:7) flows so naturally from Paul's pen in a context of practical exhortation that the idea behind it must have been taken for granted as part of Christian belief.

Paul is also our earliest witness to the idea of Christ as sin offering: 2 Cor 5:21, "For our sake he [God] made him [Christ] to be sin [i.e., sin offering] who knew no sin, so that in him we might become the righteousness of God." Gal 3:13, "Christ redeemed us from the curse of the law, having become a curse for us—for it is written, 'cursed be every one who hangs on a tree'—that in Christ Jesus the blessing of Abraham might come upon the Gentiles, that we might receive the promise of the Spirit through faith." Rom 8:3, "Sending his own Son in the likeness of sinful flesh and for sin [or: as a sin offering] he condemned sin in the flesh" (cf. also Rom 3:24-25). The second occurrence of the word "sin" in 2 Cor 5:21 contains, together with the normal meaning of moral transgression, the further meaning of sin offering (as is suggested by the fact that the Hebrew word for "sin," ḥaṭṭāʾt, also means "sin offering"). Gal 3:13 closely parallels 2 Cor 5:21. "In the likeness of sinful flesh" in Rom 8:3 is also a technical term which the Septuagint uses to translate "sin offering." Finally, "expiation by his blood" in Rom 3:24-25 (cf. also 5:6-11) is, in the religious context we have been unfolding, obviously talking about Christ as a sin offering.[8]

Thus, Christ's sacrificial redemptive activity, especially his death, is seen under the aspect of two particular sacrifices, the Passover and the sin offering, the two rites which the Jews of New Testament times associated most closely with redemption and forgiveness. In the light of early Christian convictions that

8. See especially L. Sabourin, *Rédemption Sacrificielle: Une Enquête Exégétique;* (Studia II; Brussels/Montreal: Desclée, 1961) and "Christ Made 'Sin' (2 Cor 5:21): Sacrifice and Redemption in the History of a Formula," part III, in S. Lyonnet and L. Sabourin, *Sin, Redemption and Sacrifice: A Biblical and Patristic Study* (AnBib 48; Rome: Pontifical Biblical Institute, 1970) 187-296.

the saving rites of the Old Testament were fulfilled and superseded in the person of Jesus, it was perfectly natural for them to
look upon him as both their Passover and their sin offering.

The Christians as the New Temple[9]

Paul mixes metaphors freely in speaking of this mystery of
God's presence in our lives. He describes the Christian community as a *plant* (1 Cor 3:6–9), then as a *building* (1 Cor 3:9–
15), all the while calling it the temple of God or of the Spirit (cf.
also 1 Cor 6:19; 2 Cor 6:16). "Do you not know [a phrase Paul
uses to recall something already known and accepted by his
readers] that you are God's temple and that God's spirit dwells
in you? If anyone destroys God's temple, God will destroy him.
For God's temple is holy, and that temple you are" (1 Cor 3:16–
17; cf. also 1 Cor 6:15 and 19; 2 Cor 6:16).

Paul sometimes does not clearly distinguish between the individual and the whole community as God's temple, and he also
seems to presume that his readers share his view that there is a
connection between the community or individual as temple and
the indwelling of the Spirit. This "new temple" theology is thus
part of the interpretative background for the many texts which
speak of the indwelling of the Spirit (Rom 5:5; 8:9, 11, 15–16;
1 Thess 4:8; 1 Cor 2:10–16; 2 Cor 1:22). This theology is also
found in the Pastorals (1 Tim 3:15; 2 Tim 2:20–22; Titus 2:14),
but its fullest expression is found in the deutero-Pauline corpus:

> So then you are no longer strangers and sojourners, but you are
> fellow citizens with the saints and members of the household of
> God, built upon the foundation of the apostles and prophets,
> Christ Jesus himself being the cornerstone, in whom the whole
> structure is joined together and grows into a holy temple in the
> Lord; in whom you also are built into it for a dwelling place of
> God in the Spirit. (Eph 2:19–22)

The best guidelines for interpreting this passage are 1 Cor 3:5–17,
which speaks from a somewhat different viewpoint, and Eph
4:11–16, which gives the same message while using only the
metaphor of the body. The passage addresses Gentile Christians

9. See especially McKelvey, *The New Temple*, 92–124.

who are now no longer outsiders but full members of God's household. They are told that they are being built (cf. 1 Cor 3:9–10) upon the foundation of the apostles and (NT) prophets with Jesus Christ as the cornerstone. This image marvelously complements the image of Christ as the head of the body (cf. Eph 1:22; 2:16; 3:6; 4:4, 11–16; 5:23–24). The idea of *growth* ("grows into a holy temple in the Lord") then strikingly bursts the limits of the building image, illustrating the author's freedom from convention in his attempt to express the ineffable. The further addition to this theme of the image of *living stones* in 1 Pet 2:5 makes the building/organic growth image one step more explicit, but it makes no essential addition to what is already contained here.

Eph 2:19–22 thus expresses two significant theological points: 1) The image of the community-as-temple describes an *inner process* or movement of the church toward holiness, a growth toward becoming the true temple which is as much an ontological as a moral reality. 2) This growth is a *continuous process*. To grow is of the essence of church; the church *is* inasmuch as it is becoming holy, becoming the temple of God "in" Christ.[10]

The Sacrifice of the Christians

In numerous texts scattered throughout his letters, Paul both explicitly and implicitly, and with a clarity beyond doubting, compares the life and death of the Christian with the sacrificial death of Christ. The way he quotes Ps 44:23, "For thy sake we are being killed all the day long; we are regarded as sheep to be slaughtered" (Rom 8:36), a text the Jewish tradition applied to the Maccabean martyrs, suggests that Paul also had the martyrdom/sacrifice theme in mind. Two similar texts—2 Cor 4:10–11, "Always carrying in the body the death of Jesus, so that the life of Jesus may be manifested in our bodies . . . ," and Gal 2:20, "I have been crucified with Christ; it is no longer I who live, but Christ who lives in me . . ."—help set the background for what

10. See H. Schlier, *Der Brief an die Epheser* (Düsseldorf: Patmos, 1965) 144.

Col 1:24 probably intended with its audacious "I complete what is lacking in Christ's afflictions for the sake of his body, that is, the church."

Paul viewed his own apostolic life and impending death in the the same way that he viewed Christ's, that is, as a personal self-offering: "Even if I am to be poured out as a libation upon the sacrificial offering of your faith" (Phil 2:17; cf. 2 Tim 4:6). He also sees almsgiving as an offering and speaks of it in the language of sacrifice: "That my service (*diakonia*) for Jerusalem may be *acceptable (euprosdektos)* to the saints" (Rom 15:31); "I am filled, having received from Epaphroditus the gifts you sent, a *fragrant offering, a sacrifice acceptable* and pleasing to God" (Phil 4:18). Each of these last two italicized phrases is a technical term which describes the acceptability of a sacrifice before God. Note the suggestion, supported by the context, that Paul sees the gifts of Epaphroditus as representing all the good works of the Christian life; and note also the startling implication, since sacrifice is due to God alone, that the recipient of these gifts is Paul himself (cf. also Phil 2:25). Startling as this may seem, it does make sound theological sense in light of the implications of the Christian-as-temple theme.

There is, thus, no doubt that the Pauline literature speaks of the life of apostleship and the Christian life in general as sacrificial. This fact is confirmed by the following great texts which are particularly rich sources for the Pauline view of the *liturgy of life*.[11]

ROMANS 12:1-2[12]

(1) I appeal to you therefore, brethren, by the mercies of God, to present (*parastanai*) your bodies (*sōmata*) as a living sacrifice,

11. Cf. especially R. Corriveau, *The Liturgy of Life: A Study of the Ethical Thought of St. Paul in His Letters to the Early Christian Communities* (Studia 25; Brussels/Montreal: Desclée, 1970).

12. The most helpful treatment is in Corriveau, *Liturgy of Life*, 155–85; the most extensive treatment is by P. Seidensticker, *Lebendiges Opfer (Röm 12,1). Ein Beitrag zur Theologie des Apostels Paulus* (NTAbh 20, 1/3; Münster: Aschendorff, 1954). The most complete and most balanced

holy and acceptable to God, which is your spiritual (*logikos*) worship. (2) Do not be conformed to this world but be transformed by the renewal of your mind, that you may prove what is the will of God, what is good and acceptable and perfect [or: what is the good and acceptable and perfect will of God].

The opening adjuration marks the transition from the earlier doctrinal part of the letter to the later pastoral part where Paul presents at length his theology of Christian life. The most significant aspect of this text is its startling combination of what had been heretofore incompatible: on the one hand, Hellenistic spiritualization, and on the other, Hebrew somatic and Christian incarnational views. On the one hand, Paul seems to have deliberately given the text a Hellenistic, perhaps even incipiently gnostic, spiritualizing flavor by using the vocabulary of the *logikē thusia* (spiritual/reasonable sacrifice) idea of Greek religious philosophy. On the other hand, he could hardly have found a more Semitically flavored word than *sōma* (body). As in the eucharistic words of institution where *sōma* signifies the total person of Jesus in his physical, bodily form, so here, *sōma* signifies the total Christian—in his/her physical, bodily state of being—the total Christian person who is already baptized into Christ (Rom 6:1–10) and has already become someone begotten by God in whom the Spirit dwells (Rom 8:14–16). This totality of the self is what Paul solemnly adjures his Christian brethren to offer to God (i.e., put at God's disposition) as a living, holy, and pleasing sacrifice. Paul thus combines the irreconcilable in order to bring out the true nature of Christian sacrifice. He combines the most elevated ethical and spiritual ideas of the Greeks with the somatic ideas of his Jewish experience and Christian existence. This enables him to reject the Hellenistic mistrust of matter and to emphasize two cardinal points of Christian faith: creation and incarnation. The rest of this passage thus falls harmoniously into place as describing Christian life in terms of cultic service— terms which, significantly, are as applicable to Christ as to the individual Christian.

---

commentary is that of O. Michel, *Der Brief an die Römer* (MeyerK 4; 4th ed.; Göttingen: Vandenhoeck & Ruprecht, 1966).

ROMANS 15:15–16[13]

(15) On some points I have written to you very boldly by way of
reminder, because of the grace given me by God (16) to be a
minister (*leitourgos*) of Christ Jesus to the Gentiles to perform
the sacrificial service (*hierourgein*) of preaching the gospel of
God, so that the offering of the Gentiles [i.e., the Gentiles = the
offering, as in Isa 66:20] may be acceptable, sanctified by the
Holy Spirit.

In their context in Romans as well as in their content, these verses
are at the heart of Paul's understanding of his own life. He sees
his apostolic mission as a "sacrificial service" which is priestly,
public, eschatological, and universal. He sees this "liturgy of
life" as charism or grace. For sacrifice is a comprehensive
process, part of which is obedient self-offering. The grace of
sacrifice comprises 1) the offering up of Jesus Christ, through God
and for us, 2) the "sacrificial service" or priestly activity of
preaching the word, and all that this entails existentially in one's
life, and 3) the obedience of faith in giving oneself to God for
the sake of one's neighbor. Finally, Paul sees this apostolic
"liturgy of life" as a comprehensive service involving the founding, building up, and maintenance of the church.[14]

FIRST EPISTLE OF PETER

1 Pet. 2:4–10[15] is the richest single source for a New Testament
theology of sacrifice. Although direct dependence on Paul seems
unlikely, it amplifies two of the three Pauline aspects of the
theology of sacrifice, the community as temple and the sacrificial
nature of Christian life, while the third aspect, the sacrifice of
Christ, remains implicitly in the background:

13. Cf. H. Schlier, "Die 'Liturgie' des apostolischen Evangeliums (Röm
15,14–21)," *Martyria Leitourgia Diakonia. Festschrift für Hermann Volk*
(Mainz: Grünewald, 1968) 247–59 and Corriveau, *Liturgy of Life*, 148–55.

14. 2 Cor 2:14–17 appears to reinforce emphatically this line of interpretation, especially where Paul speaks of his apostolic activity as "the
aroma of Christ to God," which recalls the phrase the Septuagint uses to
express the acceptability of a sacrifice before God: *osmē euōdias* (pleasing
fragrance).

15. See especially J. H. Elliott, *The Elect and the Holy: An Exegetical
Examination of 1 Peter 2:4–10 and the Phrase* βασίλειον ἱεράτευμα (NovTSup
12; Leiden: Brill, 1966).

(4) Come to him, to that living stone, rejected by men, but in God's sight chosen and precious (5) and like living stones be yourselves built into a spiritual (*pneumatikos*) house, to be a holy priesthood to offer spiritual sacrifices (*pneumatikas thusias*) acceptable to God through Jesus Christ. (6) For it stands in Scripture: [Isa 28:16] "Behold I am laying in Zion a stone, a cornerstone chosen and precious, and he who believes in him will not be put to shame." (7) To you therefore who believe, he is precious, but for those who do not believe, [Ps 117 LXX, 22] "The very stone which the builders rejected has become the head of the corner," (8) and [Isa 8:14] "A stone that will make men stumble, a rock that will make them fall"; for they stumble because they disobey the word, as they were destined to do. (9) But [Exod 19:6] you are a *chosen race,* a *royal priesthood,* a *holy nation,* God's own people, that you may declare the wonderful deeds of him who called you out of darkness into his marvelous light. (10) Once you were no people but now you are God's people; once you had not received mercy but now you have received mercy.

The Hellenistic, even gnostic-flavored imagery of vv. 1–3 (not quoted here) serve, like the similar language of Rom 12:1, to take up all that is good into the Christian perspective. Then, with vv. 4–5 we have come to the richest two verses in the entire Bible for the theology of sacrifice.

The invitation of v. 4 "Come to him" (i.e., "believe in Christ") uses the same verb that is used to describe the approach of the priest to the altar of sacrifice. The paradoxically striking image *living stone* is applied first to Christ and then to the Christian. "Rejected by men" recalls the parable of the wicked vintner (Mark 12:10 parr), but the addition of "living" and the invitation to us to become "living stones" both recalls the "living sacrifice" of Rom 12:1 and leads 1 Peter directly into the community-as-temple theme. The development beyond Paul consists chiefly in the inclusion in one image (living stones) of what Paul strove to express by the juxtaposition of images from plant growth and building construction. Theologically, the new image not only emphasizes the importance of internal dispositions; it also reinforces the central message of Romans 12: that true Christian sacrifice means putting oneself totally, body and soul, at the disposition of God and neighbor.

The house to be *built* of these living stones is *pneumatikos* (spiritual), not only in contrast to the material temple "made with hands," but also because it is the dwelling place of God's Spirit, the "place" where "spiritual" (= Christian) sacrifices are to be offered to God through Jesus Christ. Three important themes are thus combined: 1) the Christian form of cultic spiritualization, 2) the theology of acceptance, 3) the Christian principle of the mediatorship of Christ.

1 Pet 2:4–10 has also been famous as the focal point in Scripture for the doctrine of, and often fierce controversies concerning, universal priesthood. But this idea is not an innovation with 1 Peter; it is present in Exod 19:6: "You shall be to me a kingdom of priests and a holy nation," and is extensively alluded to in Jewish biblical and extra-biblical literature (e.g., Isa 56:6–7; 59:21; 60:7, 11; 61:6; 2 Macc 2:17; *Jub.* 16:18; 33:10; and in Philo, *de Vita Mosis* II 224–25; *de Specialibus Legibus* II 145).

Note carefully the functions of this universal priesthood: they are 1) the "cultic" function of offering spiritual (i.e., Christian) sacrifices (v. 5) and 2) the equally "cultic" function (recall Rom 15:16) of declaring "the wonderful deeds of him who called you out of darkness into his marvelous light" (v. 9). The second function is but one particular specification of the first; for this text, just like Heb 13:16, as we shall see below (p. 74), clearly identifies "spiritual sacrifices acceptable to God" with active commitment to living the Christian life.

THE TEMPLE AS COMMUNITY IN QUMRAN AND THE NEW TESTAMENT[16]

Most of the New Testament parallels to Qumran are found in Paul, Hebrews, and the Gospel of John,[17] mostly without notable variations. This indicates that there probably existed at one time an early stratum of Christian thought which either shared a common heritage with Qumran or was influenced by Qumran.

16. See *CS*, 256–60.
17. D. Flusser, "The Dead Sea Sect and Pre-Pauline Christianity," *Aspects of the Dead Sea Scrolls* (Scripta Hierosolymitana 4; Jerusalem: Magnes, 1958) 215–16.

For example, the most complete expressions of the community-as-temple idea found in the New Testament and Qumran parallel each other in a way that cannot be explained by mere coincidence but only by some form of literary relationship, as illustrated below:[18]

1 Peter 2:5–6	Qumran
and like living stones be yourselves built into	cf. 4QFlor 1:6: to build him a sanctuary of [or: "among"] men
a spiritual house	a House of Holiness for Israel—1QS 8:5 (cf. 5:6; 9:6)
	a House of Perfection and Truth in Israel—1QS 8:9
to be a holy priesthood	it shall be a Holy of Holies for Aaron—1QS 8:8–9
	an assembly of the Holy of Holies for Aaron—1QS 8:9
to offer spiritual sacrifices acceptable to God	shall offer up sweet fragrance—1QS 8:9
	they shall be an agreeable offering pleasing to God—1QS 8:6
through Jesus Christ. For it stands in scripture	
Behold, I am laying in Zion a chosen stone	it shall be that tried wall—1QS 8:7
a precious cornerstone	that precious cornerstone—1QS 8:7
and he who believes in him will not be put to shame	whose foundation shall neither rock nor sway—1QS 8:8

Further, in 2 Cor 6:16, "What agreement has the temple of God with idols? For we are the temple of the living God," there are five elements which suggest Qumran contacts: 1) the triple dualism of uprightness/iniquity, light/darkness, Christ/Beliar; 2) the opposition to idols; 3) the concept of the community as temple; 4) the separation from impurity; 5) the concatenation of Old Testament texts. The cumulative effect forms a strong case that 2 Cor 6:16, whether genuinely Pauline or an interpolation, has reworked Qumran ideas and expressions into a Christian cast of thought.[19]

18. D. Flusser, "The Dead Sea Sect," pp. 215–16.
19. Cf. J. Fitzmyer, "Qumran and the Interpolated Paragraph in 2 Cor ,14–7,1" *CBQ* 23 (1961) 271–80.

These two comparisons suggest that we have here not just parallels and analogues, but a specifically Christian reworking of Qumran ideas not known to us from any other source in the ancient world. This community-as-temple theme from Qumran is thus one of the many elements from various sources which Christianity, in becoming itself, managed to take over, assimilate, and form into something at once both strongly traditional and totally new: the religion of Jesus Christ.

THE EPISTLE TO THE HEBREWS[20]

Although Hebrews treats sacrifice more extensively than any other New Testament writing, its unparalleled uniqueness cautions against making it alone, rather than Paul, the basis for a New Testament theology of sacrifice. The "new temple" theme is totally absent; the "sacrifice-of-Christ" theme is presented primarily under the unique guise of Christ's high-priestly self-offering; while the "sacrifice-of-the-Christian" theme, quite Pauline in its thrust, is increasingly prominent in the final exhortatory part of the letter. Passover themes are notably absent and eucharistic ideas, if at all present, are far in the background (cf. *CS*, 262–63).

The basic message of Hebrews is the inefficacy of the Old Testament sacrifices as opposed to the real efficacy of the once-for-all sacrifice of Christ which alone can "perfect the conscience of the worshiper" (Heb 9:9). The specific sacrificial theme which dominates is that of Christ the eternal high priest and fulfiller of the Old Testament cult. Particularly central is the sin offering of the Day of Atonement liturgy.

This helps explain the appropriateness of the Melchizedek tradition (cf. especially Heb 7:11–19) in buttressing the basic mes-

---

20. See *CS*, 261–85. The best critical commentary on Hebrews is O. Michel, *Der Brief an die Hebräer* (MeyerK 13; 6th ed.; Göttingen: Vandenhoeck & Ruprecht, 1966). The most extensive in its treatment of detail, although somewhat outdated, is C. Spicq, L'Épitre aux Hébreux (2 vols.; 3d ed.; Paris: Gabalda, vol. 1, 1952; vol. 2, 1953).

sage of the inadequacy of the old and the perfection of the new covenant in which we have as high priest Jesus, who is not descended from the (human and imperfect) lineage of the Levitical or Aaronic priesthood, but who "has become a priest . . . by the power of an indestructible life" (Heb 7:16) which gives us "a better hope . . . through which we draw near to God" (Heb 7:19).

> (13) For if the sprinkling of defiled persons with the blood of goats and bulls and with the ashes of a heifer sanctifies for the purification of the flesh, (14) how much more shall the blood of Christ, who through the eternal Spirit offered himself without blemish to God, purify your conscience from dead works to serve the living God. (Heb 9:13–14)

> (8) When he said above, "Thou hast neither desired nor taken pleasure in sacrifices and offerings and burnt offerings and sin offerings" (these are offered according to the law) (9) then he added, "Lo, I have come to do thy will." He abolishes the first order in order to establish the second. (10) And by that will we have been sanctified through the offering of the body of Jesus Christ once for all. (Heb 10:8–10)

Thus, obedience to the dead works of the law, which is powerless to forgive sins, is replaced by the new cultic principle of service (*latreuein*) to the will of the living God. The final portion of Hebrews (10:19ff.) goes on to describe this service, this liturgy of the new covenant.

The Sacrifice of Christ the High Priest

Hebrews seems to teach that Christ became high priest only with his glorification[21]—his sitting down "at the right hand of the Majesty on high" (Heb 1:3; cf. 8:1; 10:12; 12:2). As the first Melchizedek passage puts it:

> In the days of his flesh, Jesus offered up prayers and supplications, with loud cries and tears, to him who was able to save him from death, and he was heard for his godly fear. Although he was a

21. Cf. G. Schille, "Erwägungen zur Hohepriesterlehre des Hebräerbriefes," ZNW 46 (1955) 96, 109; cf. also the literature noted in CS, 264–65.

Son, he learned obedience through what he suffered; and being made perfect he became the source of eternal salvation to all who obey him, being designated by God a high priest after the order of Melchizedek. (Heb 5:7–10)

The author may well be alluding to the theme of the Suffering Messiah. In any case, this passage certainly illustrates his concern to highlight the humanity of Jesus, as do several other passages early in the letter, such as 2:14–18 and the familiar: "For we have not a high priest who is unable to sympathize with our weaknesses, but one who in every respect has been tempted as we are, yet without sinning" (Heb 4:15; cf. also 9:26; 13:12). These texts emphasize the physical reality of the incarnation and reflect the same abasement-exaltation theme as Phil 2:5–11 and Luke 24:26.

The soteriology of Hebrews is thus clearly incarnational. Yet Jesus' high-priestly service or intercession is a continuing, ongoing, heavenly, eternal reality. Both the historical and meta-historical aspects of Christ's intercession for us are present in Hebrews, but the author did not always take pains to keep clear the distinction between them. There are also several passages (see esp. 9:18–22) which suggest that the author was either ignorant of or not overly concerned with some of the details of the specific Old Testament rites which he mentions. This contributes to the impossibility of distinguishing precisely where image and reality coincide or separate in the author's mind. Like Paul, he was apparently less concerned with logical consistency than with the attempt to communicate something of the ineffable mystery of Christ. It is well to keep this in mind as we summarize the central thought of Hebrews on the sacrifice of Christ.

Jesus redeemed us by offering himself to God as a sin offering in the full, realistic, Old Testament sense of the word. Jesus was the priest, the high priest according to the order of Melchizedek, signifying in himself the end of the Old Testament priesthood and its fulfillment. Jesus the high priest was also the offering as well as the offerer in the new cult. He carried out this sacrifice—

perfectly, once-for-all, fulfilling and superseding all other sacrifices—physically as well as spiritually (i.e., in obedience to the will of God).

Thus, following the model of Yom Kippur (Day of Atonement; cf. Lev 16), Jesus, the eternal high priest, entered the eternal sanctuary (i.e., before the presence of God) once and for all, not with the blood of bulls and goats, but with his own blood, there to make atonement for all by a single, perfect offering. He then took his place seated in glory at the right hand of God where he continues to intercede for us (cf. Heb 7:25–8:7; 9:6–14, 23–28; 10:12–22; 12:18–24).

The Sacrifice of the Christian

The central paraenetic or exhortatory purpose of Hebrews can be thus expressed: Since Christ the high priest offered himself *for our sakes* (2:9; 5:1; 6:20; 7:25; 9:24; 10:12), we should not hesitate to *"draw near."* The key phrase is "draw near," a cultic technical term signifying the priestly action of approaching the altar in order to offer sacrifice. This exhortation to "draw near with confidence to the throne of grace, that we may receive mercy and find grace to help in time of need" (4:16) is addressed repeatedly to *all* the readers of the letter (see also 7:25; 10:1; 12:18, 22–24, as well as 10:22 to which we will shortly give more attention).

In these "draw near" texts are three themes important for the the New Testament theology of sacrifice: 1) the idea, despite repeated emphasis on the once-for-all aspect of Christ's sacrifice, of the continuation (at least of the effects) of Jesus' high-priestly ministry: ". . . since he always lives to make intercession for them" (Heb 7:25; cf. also 2:18; 4:15; 8:3, 6; 9:24–28; 12:24). Hebrews is unable, or perhaps just unconcerned, to resolve this apparent contradiction. 2) Universal priesthood, while not expressed as directly as in Rom 12:1; 15:15–16; or 1 Pet 2:4–10, is nevertheless strongly implied both in the just mentioned concept of "drawing near" as well as in the concept of spiritualization. 3) Hebrews spiritualizes sacrifice in the same way Paul does. In fact, Heb 10:19ff. serves the same structural function as Rom 12:1–2: transition from the earlier largely doctrinal to the later largely practical part of the letter:

> (19) Therefore, brethren, since we have confidence to enter the sanctuary by the blood of Jesus, (20) by the new and living way which he opened for us through the curtain, that is, through his flesh, (21) and since we have a great high priest over the house of God, (22) let us *draw near* with a true heart in full assurance of faith, with our hearts sprinkled clean from an evil conscience and our bodies washed with pure water. (23) Let us hold fast the confession of our hope without wavering, for he who promised is faithful; (23) and let us consider how to stir up one another to love and good works, (25) not neglecting to meet together, as is the habit of some, but encouraging one another, and all the more as you see the Day drawing near. (Heb 10:19–25)

After the solemn exhortation to "draw near," that is, to participate in Christ's high-priestly (sacrificial) activity, vv. 23–25 spell out what this activity of "Christian sacrifice" is: it is the Christian life itself lived in community. Living the Christian life has taken over the atoning function of the sacrificial cult. Thus the deliberate sin of Heb 10:26 for which "there no longer remains a sacrifice for sins" would seem to be the separating of oneself from the only sacrificial action that now has any validity: Christian life itself.

Two chapters later (chap. 12) we come to the powerful passage in which the awesome and forbidding phenomena of Old Testament theophanies (vv. 18–19) are contrasted with four pairs of realities in the heavenly Jerusalem (vv. 22–24) described in a tone of joyous eschatological expectation. A distinct flavor of "realized" eschatology is present, so much so, in fact, that the barriers between heaven and earth seem to be dispelled, allowing us to speak of a "cultic" community of saints:

> (18) For you have not come to what may be touched, a blazing fire, and darkness, and gloom, and a tempest, (19) and the sound of a trumpet, and a voice whose words made the hearers entreat that no further messages be spoken to them. (20) For they could not endure the order that was given, "If even a beast

touches the mountain, it shall be stoned." (21) Indeed, so terrifying was the sight that Moses said, "I tremble with fear." (22) But you have come to Mount Zion and to the city of the living God, the heavenly Jerusalem, and to innumerable angels in festal gathering, (23) and to the assembly of the firstborn who are enrolled in heaven, and to a judge who is God of all, and to the spirits of just men made perfect, (24) and to Jesus, the mediator of a new covenant, and to the sprinkled blood that speaks more graciously than the blood of Abel. (Heb 12:18–24)

Then, after 12:25–27 has exhorted us, in the context of expectation for an imminent parousia, to listen carefully to the voice of the "sprinkled blood," we are exhorted to the worship of the new covenant: "Therefore let us be grateful for receiving a kingdom that cannot be shaken, and thus let us offer [or: "in that we offer"] to God acceptable worship with reverence and awe" (Heb 12:28). Chapter 13 immediately specifies this cultic "program" with a series of exhortations to the practice of Christian virtue. Once again the practical living of the Christian life is spoken of as sacrificial:

(10) We have an altar from which those who serve the tent have no right to eat. (11) For the bodies of those animals whose blood is brought into the sanctuary by the high priest as a sacrifice for sin are burned outside the camp. (12) So Jesus also suffered outside the gate in order to sanctify the people through his own blood. (13) Therefore let us go forth to him outside the camp, bearing abuse for him. (14) For here we have no lasting city, but we seek the city which is to come. (15) Through him then let us continually offer up a sacrifice of praise to God, that is, the fruit of lips that acknowledge his name. (16) Do not neglect to do good and to share what you have, for such sacrifices are pleasing to God. (Heb 13:10–16)[22]

Opinion has divided, often along confessional lines, about whether this passage is speaking about the Eucharist. The most satisfying answer is that eucharistic meaning is probably present but clearly not as the central intention of this passage, for the

22. Michel, *Der Brief an die Hebräer*, 485–87, 498–526, is especially detailed in its treatment of these verses. On the question of the Eucharist in Hebrews, see *CS*, 262–63; 281–82.

author seems to have in mind the total saving action of Christ. "Altar" in v. 10 signifies at least the spiritualized equivalent of a sacrificial ritual. The exhortatory transition in v. 13, just like those of Rom 12:1 and Heb 10:19ff. (see above, pp. 63–64 and 73) introduces the concrete specification of Christian sacrifice in practical terms (vv. 15–16; cf. 10:23–24; 12:28). "Fruit of lips" is fairly common in Old Testament and Jewish literature as a symbolic metaphor of worthy worship. But only in Qumran (1QS 9 and 10) does it have so explicit a sacrificial meaning as in Heb 13:15. Not surprisingly, Qumran also provides the strongest pre-Christian Jewish witness to the spiritualized concept of sacrifice as the practical life of virtue.

Finally, these three major Christian-life-as-sacrifice texts (Heb 10:19–25; 12:18–28; 13:10–16) share a similar structure or pattern of thought: first, the idea of the Old Testament cult (12:18–21 = 13:10b–11) being superseded by the New Testament cult in which the believer also is exhorted to take part (12:22–24 = 13: 10a and 12–13); second, exhortation or supporting reasons presented in the context of expectation for the parousia (12:25–27 = 13:14); third, direct exhortation to the believers to offer spiritualized sacrifices (12:28 = 13:15). This pattern, which has a slightly different order in 10:19–25, probably represents a characteristic way of preaching in the primitive church. It is thus a further confirmation that the thought within the pattern is not peculiar to Hebrews (and Paul) but is instead characteristic of primitive Christianity.

In conclusion, although a great deal of what is in the Epistle to the Hebrews is not found elsewhere in the New Testament, there is nothing in it which cannot readily harmonize with Paul's theology of sacrifice. Like Paul, Hebrews clearly presents Christian life as a spiritualized sacrifice. Paul's vision is broader, for he sees not only the virtuous life as an offering to God, but also his own apostolic and missionary endeavor as a priestly sacrificial ministry. On the other hand, Hebrews shows far more clearly than Paul the derivation of the sacrifice of the Christian from the once-for-all sacrifice of Christ, and the dependence of the Christian's sacrifice upon Christ's continuing high-priestly mediation.

THE GOSPEL AND FIRST LETTER OF JOHN[23]

Temple Themes

The theology of Christian community as the new temple is far more advanced in the Johannine literature than in the Synoptics. "The Word . . . dwelt [pitched his tent] among us" (John 1:14), in its allusion to the desert tent of meeting, which eventually became the Most Holy Place of the temple, suggests the end of the temple. John's account of the cleansing of the temple (2:13–22) heightens its cultic flavor by placing the event at Passover time, by mentioning animals used for sacrifice, and by Jesus calling the temple a house of prayer. Jesus' words to the Samaritan woman about true worship "in spirit and truth" (John 4:23–24) announce the beginning of the liberation of worship from a particular place. We must not forget, as we shall see shortly, that the spiritualization at work here is really a "Christologization," and that "in spirit and truth" is not far in meaning from the Pauline "in Christ."

Two further texts contain unique Johannine allusions to the temple. The incident in John 7:37–38 took place at the Feast of Tabernacles (the temple dedication). In a special ceremony, water from the pool of Siloam and wine were poured into two bowls on the altar. At the dramatic moment, the priest removed plugs from the bottom of the bowls so that wine and water flowed out, the wine into a special receptacle, the water through sluices under the altar to the "Stone of Foundation" which was in Hebrew legend the first solid thing created by God, the navel of the world from under which flows life-giving water to the whole earth. This is the context of Jesus' cry: "If any one thirst let him come to me and drink. He who believes in me, as the scripture

---

23. See CS, 286–307. Exegetes generally agree that the two works are from the same hand. For the Gospel, I have relied primarily on R. E. Brown, *The Gospel According to John* (2 vols.; AB 29; New York: Doubleday, 1966–70) and R. Schnackenburg, *Das Johannesevangelium* (3 vols. HTKNT IV/1-3; Freiburg/Vienna, 1967–75); for the First Letter, on R. Schnackenburg, *Die Johannesbriefe* (HTKNT XIII/3; Freiburg/Vienna, 1953).

has said, 'Out of his heart shall flow rivers of living water.' "
Then, in view of the centrality of the temple theme in John, the
blood and water from Christ's side at the crucifixion and the
evangelist's emphatic affirmation of the eyewitness-truth of what
he has seen (19:34–35) could not but recall what Jesus had pro-
claimed on the Feast of Tabernacles. John's witness in 19:35
pushes us to a clearer awareness that Jesus is the new temple,
that he alone is now the source of living water (i.e., faith), and
that by drinking (believing in Jesus) we also become sources of
living water for others. Thus we have in these two passages a
uniquely Johannine allusion to the Pauline image of the Chris-
tian(s) as temple of God.[24]

Sacrificial Self-Giving

The idea of *sacrificial self-giving*, especially in the *"hyper"-
formulas* (for you, for us), runs through the Johannine literature.
Among many examples are John 3:16: the love which motivates
the Father to give his only Son; 10:11, 15: the Good Shepherd
giving his life for his sheep, and 10:17 stressing that this sacrificial self-giving is both perfectly voluntary and done in loving
obedience to God; 13:1–15 interpreting the washing of the feet
as an act of service *for us*, impelling us to do the same *for the
brethren*; 11:49–52 and 18:14 recording Caiaphas' "prophecy" that
it was expedient that one man should die for the people; 15:13
speaking of the supreme act of love of giving one's life for one's
friends; and finally, the exhortation of 1 John 3:16 to imitate
Christ's sacrificial self-giving: "By this we know love, that he
laid down his life for us; and we ought to lay down our lives for
the brethren" (cf. also 1 John 4:10–11). Thus the same intimate
association between the sacrifice of Christ and the sacrifice of the
Christian which we found in Paul and Hebrews is also richly
witnessed to in the Johannine writings.

24. Cf. Mishnah *Sukkah* 4:1 and 9 (Danby, *Mishnah*, 177–79); R. Patai,
Man and Temple (New York: KTAV, 1947; repr. 1967) 24–53; Brown,
The Gospel According to John, 1. 319–27; G. W. MacRae, "The Meaning
and Evolution of the Feast of Tabernacles," *CBQ* 22 (1960) 251–76.

Sin Offering and Atonement Themes

These figure prominently in John's first letter. Typical of these passages is 1 John 2:1-2: ". . . but if any one does sin, we have an advocate with the Father, Jesus Christ the righteous; and he is the expiation (*hilasmos*) for our sins, and not for ours only but also for the sins of the whole world" (see also 1 John 1:7 and 4:10). These passages are similar to a number of Pauline texts (2 Cor 5:21; Gal 3:13; Rom 3:24; 8:3; see above, p. 60). Whether *hilasmos* in a neologism for sin offering, or means atonement in general, or both, is not the central question. For what provides the immediate background is the early rabbinic concept of sin offering and atonement rites, strongly colored by the idea of the vicarious sufferings and death of the just man and the martyr.

John too, like Paul, sees Christ as the Paschal sacrifice and emphasizes far more than the Synoptics that Christ's death is a Passover event. Christ's death and resurrection occur at the third of the three Passovers with which John frames his Gospel, and he also locates the hour of death at the very time when the Passover lambs were being slaughtered at the temple (John 19:14, 31). The use of hyssop (in 19:29) instead of the synoptic *kalamos* recalls the blood rite of the Egyptian Passover (Exod 12:22). Finally, John 19:36, "Not a bone of him shall be broken" (from the regulations of preparation for the Paschal lambs [cf. Exod 12:46; Num 9:12; Ps 34:20]), sets up a direct comparison between the crucified Christ and the Paschal lamb.

THE HISTORY-OF-RELIGIONS CONTEXT OF "WORSHIP IN SPIRIT AND IN TRUTH"[25]

This concerns above all Jesus' words to the Samaritan woman: "But the hour is coming, and now is, when true worshipers will worship the Father in spirit and truth, for such the Father seeks

25. Qumran provides an illuminating background: 1QS 3:6–8; 4:20–21; 9:3–6; 1QH 16:11–12; 17:26. Cf. Schnackenburg, *Johannesevangelium* 1:471–74; "Die 'Anbetung in Geist und Wahrheit' (Joh 4,23) im Lichte von Qumran-Texten," *BZ* n.f. 3 (1959) 88–94; B. Gärtner, *The Temple and the Community in Qumran and the New Testament* (SNTSMS 1; New York/London: Cambridge University, 1965) 18–21, 44–46, 84–87, 119–20; O. Cullmann, "L'opposition contre le temple de Jerusalem, motif commun

to worship him. God is spirit, and those who worship him must worship in spirit and truth" (John 4:23–24). One of the favorite presuppositions of the earlier study of comparative religions was its understanding of spiritualization, that is, that a religion approaches perfection to the extent that it is free of material (or even social) elements. The insight that true (i.e., spiritual) worship derives from the nature of God as pure spirit was seen as a contribution of Greek religious philosophy. But to see here the source of the Judeo-Christian or Johannine idea of "worship in spirit and in truth" is a massive misunderstanding. For the awareness of God as "spirit" and the superiority and absolute necessity of spiritual (i.e., internal, or performed with proper religious-ethical dispositions) over merely external worship became well established in Judaism and Christianity for the most part independently of Hellenistic influence. Furthermore, "spirit" and "truth" in John 4:23–24 are so thoroughly christological that we must bring to bear on this passage the full force of John's antidocetic, incarnational, even "sacramental" Christology. Spiritualization in the classical, antimaterial sense ignores the basic meaning of this passage in its Johannine context. For the main point here is that true worship is in no sense a human work; it can never be done in the flesh (i.e., by merely human means) but only in the spirit (i.e., in Christ), with the help of God "from above" (cf. John 3:3, 7, 31; 6:44; 9:11).

THE BOOK OF REVELATION[26]

From 4:1 to the epilogue (22:6) this book is a series of visions of the heavenly sanctuary seen after the model of the Jerusalem

de la théologie johannique et du monde ambiant," *NTS* 5 (1958–59) 157–73; R. Bultmann, *Das Evangelium des Johannes* (MeyerK 2; 10th ed.; Göttingen: Vandenhoeck & Ruprecht, 1962) 140 n. 3; H. Wenschkewitz, "Die Spiritualisierung der Kultusbegriffe. Tempel, Priester und Opfer im Neuen Testament," *Angelos* 4 (1932) 220–21.

26. See *CS*, 295–307. Cf. E.-B. Allo, *L'Apocalypse* (4th ed.; Paris: Gabalda, 1933); W. Bousset, *Die Offenbarung Johannis* (MeyerK 16; 6th ed.; Göttingen: Vandenhoeck & Ruprecht, 1906, repr. 1966); A. Wikenhauser, *Die Offenbarung des Johannes* (RNT 9; 3d ed.; Regensburg: Pustet, 1959); E. Lohmeyer, *Die Offenbarung des Johannes* (HNT 16 2d ed.; Tübingen: Mohr, 1953).

temple. The seer, taken up "in the spirit" (4:1), finds himself outside the sanctuary, aparently in the vicinity of or in line with the altar of sacrifice (which he does not mention), looking into the Most Holy Place where the throne of God is situated. This is at least the starting point for all the visions in Revelation:

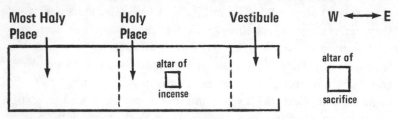

The Throne of God

The throne of God, almost identified with God himself as in Hebrews (4:16; 8:1; 12:2), is the center of the visions. But unlike Hebrews, Revelation concentrates entirely on worship in the heavenly sanctuary or, after the millennium, in the new Jerusalem. Many have noted how closely Rev 3:21, "He who conquers, I will grant him to sit with me on my throne, as I myself conquered [cf. John 16:33] and sat down with my Father on his throne," parallels Luke 22:30, ". . . that you may eat and drink at my table in my kingdom, and sit on thrones. . . ." But few have remarked how thoroughly Johannine Rev 3:21 is in thought and expression; for it teaches that Jesus' followers are given the same mission and power and glory which Jesus himself shares with the Father (cf. John 6:57; 13:12–15; 17:7–10, 20–26; 20:21–23).

The Lamb

"The Lamb" with soteriological and messianic connotations is the most frequent christological title (twenty-eight occurrences) in Revelation.[27] The several references to the Lamb as slain (Rev 5:6, 9, 12; 13:8) also make it an obvious sacrificial symbol. The sacrificial meaning is reinforced by the further references to the *blood of the Lamb* which is seen in some texts as the source of

27. Cf. A. Läpple, *Die Apokalypse nach Johannes* (Munich: Don Bosco Verlag, 1966) 201; J. Jeremias, *"arnion," TDNT* 1 (1964) 338–41.

the martyr's strength: "And they conquered him [i.e., the accuser of our brethren (12:10)] by the blood of the Lamb and by the word of their testimony, for they loved not their lives even unto death" (cf. also Rev 7:14; 1:5). With such a variety of evidence there is no doubt that the Lamb of the Apocalypse is the crucified and glorified Lord who appears now in heaven in the form of a sacrificial lamb.

The descriptions of the Lamb as "slain" suggest a Passover background, and the various occurrences of the "blood of the Lamb" suggest a sin offering background. But without excluding either of these, the idea of the Lamb as Servant of God seems easily the most satisfying. For not only are there verbal similarities between the Fourth Servant Song of Isaiah 53 and the Lamb-as-slain texts of Revelation, and not only does the same Aramaic word *talya'*, which means servant as well as lamb, probably underlie the two New Testament words for lamb,[28] but also and most significantly, of these three background possibilities only the Servant of God is a personal title capable of carrying the full breadth of christological meaning associated with the title: the Lamb.

The Incense Offering

"And when he had taken the scroll, the four living creatures and twenty-four elders fell down before the Lamb, each holding a harp, and with golden bowls full of incense, which are the prayers of the saints" (Rev 5:8; cf. also 8:1–4) is the only concrete Jewish sacrificial ceremony directly mentioned in Revelation. This is due probably to the Christian aversion to cultic sacrifice as well as to the ease with which the incense offering could be spiritualized. In fact, the altar of sacrifice is not even mentioned in Revelation; the one altar of incense, within the Holy Place, seems to serve for both (cf. 6:9; 8:3, 5; 9:13; 14:18; 16:7). Finally, early Christianity seems to be dependent on Judaism for its close association of the idea of the altar of incense with the prayers of the souls of the martyrs and saints (cf., e.g.,

28. J. Jeremias and W. Zimmerli, *"pais theou," TDNT* 5 (1967) 700.

the idea of martyrdom as a sacrificial offering as stated in Phil 2:17 and 2 Tim 4:6).

In conclusion then, although Revelation uses the same basic imagery of the heavenly liturgy as Hebrews, the two works are worlds apart. Hebrews is very much a this-worldly book. Even while attempting to plumb the depths of the mystery of Christ, the eternal mediator and high priest, it never moves far from the practical concerns of the real, down-to-earth Christian life. But Revelation never descends from the heavenly sanctuary, except at the end to speak of the new Jerusalem which will come down out of heaven at the millennium (Rev 21:1–22:5). Thus, although much is said that can be related to various aspects of the New Testament and the early Christian theology of sacrifice, and although most of the work describes a heavenly liturgy which is, at least by implication, sacrificial, the Book of Revelation actually adds very little to the Christian theology of sacrifice.

SUMMARY

The theology of sacrifice of the New Testament writers, and consequently the sacrificial soteriology of the New Testament and early church, fits readily into the threefold Pauline division: 1) the sacrifice of Christ, 2) the Christian(s) as the new temple, 3) the sacrifice(s) of the Christians. However, our most significant finding is not the hitherto neglected convenience of this division, but rather the strength of the evidence we discover that the third of these divisions, the sacrifices which Christians offer, has primarily an ethical rather than ritual or liturgical meaning. There is a long and controversy-laden history to the idea that Christian sacrifice, or, more generally, true Christian worship, is centered not in acts of ritual and liturgical worship but in the practical, ethical sphere of the lived Christian life. The idea as such is not new. What is new, and what establishes the necessary starting-point for all future reflection on the meaning of Christian sacrifice, is our demonstration that the commonly accepted methods of modern critical scholarship prove beyond reasonable doubt that this primarily ethical concept of Christian sacrifice is indeed the one that is operative in the New Testament.

The consistency of this conclusion with the development of the idea of Israelite and Christian sacrifice sketched in this work can also be forcefully demonstrated by examining that handful of New Testament passages which speak of the sacrifices offered by Christians: Rom 12:1–2; Rom 15:15–16; 1 Pet 2:4–10; Heb 10:19–25; 12:18–13:16. In each of these passages, either explicitly or implicitly (from the fact that they all occur in the context of practical exhortation), sacrifice is understood as the practical living of the life of Christian virtue and Christian mission. The core of the specifically New Testament concept of Christian sacrifice is, thus, not cultic or liturgical, but practical and ethical. The sacrifice to be offered by the people of God in the new covenant is indeed a *liturgy of life*.[29]

29. Precisely what this study claims to be able to prove is that true Christian sacrifice is centered *primarily*—but not necessarily exclusively—in the ethical sphere rather than in the ritual or ceremonial sphere of life. There is nothing in these findings which, properly understood, should suggest that liturgical worship is unnecessary or unessential. For, although my own theological position and religious conviction affirm that public worship is an essential Christian obligation and an essential part of Christian sacrifice, it is not the purpose of this book to present the specific warrants for this position. I claim, as demonstrably true, that Christian worship-sacrifice is always and necessarily rooted in ethical or practical self-giving to others; I leave open, on the basis of this study, whether or to what extent ethical self-giving to others is, conversely, also rooted in the Christian's worship-sacrifice.

CHAPTER FIVE

THE EARLY CHURCH

The faith, the practice, and the writings of the early Christians have usually been looked upon as being in some sense normative for the faith and practice of later Christians. Even those who are reluctant to grant such status to the patristic age have to admit the importance of the Fathers both as interpreters of biblical revelation and as keys to understanding the faith and theology of later ages. Until recently, most patristic research on confessionally sensitive topics such as sacrifice has been, at worst, blatant "proof-texting" and at best, influenced by unconscious confessional or polemical bias. Now, however, aided by the expanded resources of modern scholarship, and somewhat liberated from the polemics of the past, we can hope that a fresh look at the early church's concepts of sacrifice will prove illuminating for the present. Methodologically, we will be watching to see whether and to what extent the Pauline triple division of sacrificial themes (sacrifice of Christ, the new temple, sacrifice of Christians) is a helpful focus of analysis. Thematically, we will be paying close attention 1) to the spiritualization of sacrifice, and 2) to the relationship between the Eucharist and sacrifice.

THE EARLY WRITINGS

In the Didache,[1] the four allusions to Jesus as servant in the eucharistic hymns of chapters 9 and 10 may be implicitly sacrifi-

1. A brief Greek document called The Teaching of the Twelve Apostles from the end of the first or beginning of the second century A.D. It appears to be the earliest extant church order. Most readily accessible translation in J. A. Kleist, *The Apostolic Fathers* (Ancient Christian Writers 6; Washington: The Catholic University of America Press, 1948).

cial. But more significant is the way Didache 14 calls the Sunday liturgy a sacrifice:

> On the Lord's Day assemble together to break bread and offer thanks, after first confessing your sins, so that your sacrifice may be pure. But no one quarreling with his brother may join your meeting until they are reconciled, so that your sacrifice may not be defiled. For on this matter we have the Lord's word: [Mal 1:11] "In every place and time offer me a pure sacrifice; for I am a mighty King, says the Lord; and my name spreads terror among the nations." (*Did.* 14:1-3)

There are obvious similarities with Matt 5:23-24 and the early rabbinic ideal of confession when bringing a sacrifice for sin to the altar (see above, pp. 29 and 54). But most importantly, the quotation of Mal 1:11 (as a command instead of a prophecy) suggests that the author is at home with the idea of the Eucharist as sacrifice.

Clement of Rome's views on sacrifice in his Epistle to the Romans (around A.D. 96) comprise three points. First, in words suggestive both of the theology of divine acceptance (7:3-4) and of the philosophical criticism of sacrifice (52:1-4), and by stressing the obedience of Abraham and Isaac in their sacrifice (10:7; 31:3), he emphasizes that *true sacrifice is according to the will of God.* Second, he spiritualizes sacrifice by placing in emphatic positions at the end of chapters 18, 35, and 52 carefully selected excerpts from some of the spiritualizing psalm texts (e.g., note how, in chap. 35, he ends his quotation of [LXX] Ps 49:17-23 at the words: "The sacrifice of praise will glorify me"). Third, in a manner that is unique among the early Fathers, he institutionalizes Christian sacrifice within the liturgical life of the church. *1 Clem.* 40:1-5 appeals to the old law to justify strict regulation of the times, places, and ministers of the church's worship. He then gives a startling reformulation of Mal 1:11[2] going directly against the very popular early Christian reading of it as a prophecy of the new Christian cult unrestricted by time and place.

---

2. "For from the rising of the sun, even to its setting, my name is great among the nations, and everywhere they bring sacrifice to my name, and a pure offering; for great is my name among the nations, says the Lord of hosts" (Mal 1:11).

We can only surmise that Clement apparently wanted to counter-act what he perceived to be anti-institutional abuses or tendencies in the church. "Not in every place, brethren, are the daily sac-rifices offered, . . . but in Jerusalem only. And even there they are not offered in any place, but only at the altar before the temple" (*1 Clem.* 41:2).

Later, Clement indicates that the characteristic function of the priestly office is to offer sacrifice (*1 Clem.* 44:3–4). But precisely what Clement means by "offer the sacrifices" is left unclear. Nor is it clear why, almost three decades after the tem-ple's destruction (in A.D. 70), he continues to speak of temple worship in the present tense. However, the tension between spiritualization and institutionalization in Clement would not seem to be radically irreconcilable as long as we remember that spiritualization in a truly incarnational Christianity cannot be antimaterial or anti-institutional in its basic principles.

In *Ignatius of Antioch*, the threefold Pauline division becomes helpful, although the idea of Christ's sacrifice is more implicit than explicit.

Ignatius sees both the individual and community as temple of God. The image of "living stones" from 1 Pet 2:4–10 also finds a further development:

> . . . you . . . as being stones of the temple of the Father, and drawn up on high by the instrument of Jesus Christ, which is the cross, making use of the Holy Spirit as a rope, while your faith was the means by which you ascended, and your love the way which led up to God. (Ign. *Eph.* 9:1)

There is also an ecclesiastical development. For Ignatius uses the altar as an image of the church, understanding "one altar" or the state of being "within the altar" as symbols of church unity.[3]

However, Ignatius' thought lags behind Paul's in that he does not speak so explicitly of the whole of Christian life but, for the most part, only of martyrdom as sacrificial—although the intensity with which he does this is indeed unmatched: "Do not seek to confer any greater favor upon me than that I be sacrificed to God

---

3. Cf. Ign. *Eph.* 5:2; Ign. *Phld.* 4; 7:2; Ign. *Trall.* 7:2; Ign. *Magn.* 7:2.

while the altar is still prepared" (Ign. *Rom.* 2:2). "I am the wheat of God, and let me be ground by the teeth of the wild beasts, that I may be found the pure bread of Christ. . . . Entreat Christ for me, that by these instruments, I may be found a sacrifice [to God]" (Ign. *Rom.* 4:1–2).

The Shepherd of Hermas (a somewhat moralizing, allegorical work from the mid-second century, highly regarded in early Christianity) speaks of fasting as sacrifice (*Herm. Sim.* 5:3). Also, the way in which *Herm. Vis.* 3:2:4–3:7:6 speaks of the church as a tower under construction evokes the *living stones* image of 1 Pet 2:5, especially as further developed in the Ign. *Eph.* 9:1 passage quoted just above. We cannot be sure, however, that any temple symbolism was directly intended by the author.

Polycarp (bishop of Smyrna, martyred A.D. 156) just repeats the already current stock phrases of Christian piety (Pol. *Phil.* 1:2; 8:1; 9:2) except for one point. He is apparently the first Christian writer to take up the idea (which was very strong in Philo) of an individual as altar when he calls widows "the altar of God" (Pol. *Phil.* 4:3).

THE APOLOGISTS: JUSTIN AND ATHENAGORAS

Justin Martyr, in his two Apologies (A.D. 150–155) and the somewhat later Dialogue with Trypho the Jew, becomes the first Christian writer to treat sacrifice as a theological question. While insisting that Christians, in fulfillment of the Old Testament, offer real sacrifice, he is equally emphatic regarding the essential difference between Christian sacrifice and the sacrifices of the pagans and Jews which he fiercely rejects. We will treat first his anti-sacrifice polemic, then his understanding of the sacrifice of Christ, and finally his views on the sacrifice of the Christians.

Justin's *anti-sacrifice polemic* includes not merely the philosophical argument regarding the impropriety of offering material sacrifice to the spiritual God (*1 Apol.* 10:1; 13:1; *Trypho* 10:3), but also a specifically religious condemnation of sacrifice as an idolatry inspired by evil spirits: "We are persuaded that these things are prompted by evil spirits, who demand sacrifices and service even from those who live unreasonably" (*1 Apol.* 12:5; cf. also 9:1). Not altogether fairly, Justin lets this fierce anti-pagan polemic "rub off" onto the Jewish cult which he likewise castigates as idolatrous and demon-inspired (*1 Apol.* 62:1; *2 Apol.* 5:3–4), or at best, as something grudgingly tolerated by God to keep the Jews from falling into real idolatry (*Trypho* 19:3; 22:1; 92:4–5).

Despite this fiercely negative attitude, however, Justin takes from the Jewish cult much of its implicit theology, especially the *theology of divine acceptance of sacrifice.* (*1 Apol.* 37–39; *Trypho* 12:3; 15:4; 28:5; 40:4) and the idea of *atonement as the purpose of sacrifice* (*Trypho* 22:1; 40:4: 41:1; 111:3–4; 112:1–2).

As for *the sacrifice of Christ,* Justin develops a bit further the Christian tradition which, since Paul (1 Cor 5:7), saw Christ as the fulfillment of the Passover sacrifice:

> The mystery, then, of the lamb which God enjoined to be sacrificed as the Passover was the type of Christ with whose blood in proportion to their faith in him, they anoint their houses, i.e., themselves, who believe in him. . . . and that lamb which was commanded to be wholly roasted was a symbol of the suffering of the cross which Christ would undergo. (*Trypho* 40:1–2)

This typological relationship is later developed into an identity between Christ and the Passover lamb (*Trypho* 72:1) and is made even more explicit by a reference to Isa 53:7 (*Trypho* 111:3).

Justin also continues the tradition of seeing Christ as an offering for sin. He does this in his interpretation of the Leviticus 16 two-goat ritual of Yom Kippur (*Trypho* 40:4), by his famous allegorical interpretation of the scarlet thread hung out by Rahab the harlot at Jericho as symbolizing the redeeming blood of Christ (*Trypho* 111:4), and by repeatedly associating Gen 49:11 and Isa 53:7 with the sacrifice of Christ. Although most of this is recognizably Pauline, or a development of Pauline thought, it seems likely that Justin did not know Paul's writings directly. How else might we explain his failure to use the community-as-temple theme which would have marvelously aided his anti-Jewish polemic?

The *sacrifice of the Christian* is a subject on which we might expect the greatest reserve from Justin, in view of his anti-sacrifice polemic. Yet, on the contrary, he defends Christians against the charge of atheism (because they do not offer sacrifice) by insisting that they do indeed offer sacrifice, but not in such a way as to waste creatures (as does pagan sacrifice) but in such a way as to use them properly, that is, for man (*1 Apol.* 13:1). He also insists with Trypho that God "finds our sacrifices (*thusias*) more pleasing than yours" (*Trypho* 29:1).

Toward the end of this dialogue we find Justin's most important statement on sacrifice:

And so, anticipating all the sacrifices which we offer through this name, and which Jesus the Christ commanded us to offer, i.e., in the Eucharist of the bread and the cup, and which are presented by Christians in every place throughout the world [cf. Mal 1:10–11], God himself bears witness that they are pleasing to him. But he utterly rejects the sacrifices presented by you and by those priests of yours, saying, "And I will not accept your sacrifices at your hands; for from the rising of the sun to its setting my name is glorified among the Gentiles (he says); but you profane it" [Mal 1:10–12]. Yet even now in your love of contention you assert that God does not accept the sacrifices of those who then dwelt in Jerusalem and were called Israelites. But you say that he is pleased with the prayers of the individuals of that nation then dispersed, and you call their prayers sacrifices. Now, that prayers and giving thanks, when offered by worthy men, are the only perfect and pleasing sacrifices to God, I also admit. For such sacrifices are what Christians alone have undertaken to offer; and they do this in the remembrance effected by their solid and liquid food whereby the suffering endured by the Son of God is brought to mind. (*Trypho* 117:1–3)[4]

"Sacrifices which we offer" (117:1) indicates that Justin is not speaking of something abstract but of a concrete, familiar action.

---

4. The remainder of the chapter continues to stress that the Malachi prophecy can refer *only* to the prayers and giving of thanks offered by the Christians all over the earth.

He claims that these sacrifices were commanded by Jesus Christ, and then he moves on to identify them with the Eucharist. The way in which Justin, elsewhere in this dialogue (esp. 4:13), has also brought together the themes of sacrifice and Eucharist while commenting on Mal 1:10–12 leaves no room to evade the conclusion that Justin is here speaking of the Eucharist, and is speaking of it as sacrificial. Furthermore, whenever Justin tends to become more specific about sacrifice, he is speaking of the Eucharist. For Justin, Christian sacrifice is the Eucharist.

Now the question must be put: What precisely does he mean when he thinks or writes of the Eucharist as sacrifice? For it is just this kind of text that has been interpreted in very different ways by persons of different confessional backgrounds. The key appears to be in 117:2 where Justin speaks of "prayers and giving of thanks" as the "only perfect and well-pleasing sacrifices." This is consistent with what he says elsewhere in this dialogue and the two apologies. Just as the New Testament idea of sacrifice offered by Christians is primarily the spiritualized sacrifice of the practical living of Christian life, so Justin's idea of sacrifice by Christians is primarily the spiritualized sacrifice of prayer, especially in the eucharistic celebration. It does not appear that Justin extended his notion of sacrifice to include the ritual (or consecratory) action over the gifts of bread and wine. To do so would have been to put the question in a way that apparently did not occur to him, or at least did not interest him. We can only conjecture whether he would have found such an extension consistent or inconsistent with his own thought.

But who is to offer these prayers? It is obviously the "president": "Bread and wine are brought, and the president in like manner offers prayers and thanksgivings according to his ability, and the people assent, saying Amen" (1 Apol. 67:5; cf. 65:3). But who is to preside? The bishop? Could it also be a layman? Justin is certainly favorable to the idea of universal priesthood as *Trypho* 116:3 which calls Christians "the true high-priestly race of God" clearly shows. He also seems to have a positive attitude toward ministerial office. But to say more than this is to go beyond the meager evidence supplied by Justin.

From Athenagoras of Athens (about A.D. 177) we have one single but theologically rich passage which, like Justin, at first draws upon the philosophical criticism of sacrifice but then moves beyond Justin to speak of the bloodless sacrifice of spiritual (or reasonable) worship:

> As to why we do not sacrifice, the Framer and Father of this universe has no need of blood or the odor of holocausts or the fragrance of flowers and incense; for he is himself perfect fragrance and needs nothing from within or without. But for him the noblest sacrifice is to know who stretched out and vaulted the heavens, . . . What need have I of holocausts of which God has no need?—though we do indeed need to offer a bloodless sacrifice and spiritual [or: reasonable] worship (*anaimakton thusian . . . logikēn . . . latreian*). (Plea for the Christians 13)

From this it would seem that Athenagoras admitted sacrifice only in a thoroughly spiritualized sense. Further, since this text does not seem to reflect an incarnational openness to the material, as do Rom 12:1 and 1 Pet 2:5, it may not be so closely related to these as it is to the intertestamental Testament of Levi which also speaks of a "spiritual and bloodless sacrifice" in 3:6.

IRENAEUS OF LYONS

The five books of the Adversus Haereses and the smaller The Proof of the Apostolic Preaching, written by Irenaeus toward the end of the second century, contain, as did the works of Justin, a wealth of unsystematized references to sacrifice. We will concentrate on those which contain new or particularly important developments, for much of Irenaeus' thinking on this point represents traditional teaching.

He is quite traditional in his fairly extensive use of the cult criticism of the Hebrew prophets (e.g., *Adv. Haer.* IV 26:1 and 29:1-4). But he also insists, as did the philosophers and poets, that God has no need of sacrifices (*Adv. Haer.* III 12:11; IV 31:2 and 5). Then, reflecting on the Bible, he reminds us that we are the ones who need sacrifice, and that sacrifices were in fact ordained by God for our benefit. In a typical passage (which also seems to presuppose the traditional gift-theory of sacrifice) he writes:

> He himself has no need of these services but rather, wants us to offer them for our own benefit and lest we be unfruitful. This is why the Word, although he himself had no need of such things, commanded the people to offer sacrifices. It was in order that they might learn to serve God. It is also his will, therefore, that we, too, should offer a gift at the altar, frequently and unceasingly. (*Adv. Haer.* IV 31:5)

But, with Irenaeus, we have also turned an important corner. For he parts decisively from Justin in his readiness to see Old Testament sacrifices quite openly and positively as a providential preparation for Christian sacrifice. This comes forth very clearly in his teaching that the difference between Jewish and Christian sacrifice is one of "*species*," not "*genus*." For there are sacrifices now among the Christians just as there used to be among the Jews. But while the general class (*genus*) of sacrifices remains, their *species* has been changed, inasmuch as they are now offered "not by slaves but by free men. . . . For with him there is nothing purposeless or without signification or design" (*Adv. Haer.* IV 31:1).

It would be misleading, however, to suggest a massive break between Justin and Irenaeus. The differences can be accounted for by their immediate purposes: a great deal of Justin's polemic was directed against the Jews, while Irenaeus, in his struggle against the Gnostics, had to stress continually the theme of unity, especially the real continuity between the two testaments, in order to be able to demonstrate in the one Jesus Christ the keystone of comprehensive unity. "He [the Lord] did not make void, but fulfilled the law, by performing the offices of the high priest" (*Adv. Haer.* IV 16).[5] The similar ways in which, for example, Justin and Irenaeus interpret Mal 1:10–12 and Gen 49:10–12, each of them associating these texts with the incarna-

5. Cf. also *Adv. Haer.* III 18:1 and P. Smulders, *The Fathers on Christology: The Development of Christological Dogma from the Bible to the Great Councils* (trans. L. Roy; De Pere, Wis.: St. Norbert Abbey Press, 1968) 11–12.

tion through John 1:13, indicate that they are drawing upon basically the same theological tradition.[6]

The threefold Pauline division of the theology of sacrifice—the sacrifice of Christ, the temple theme, and the sacrifice of Christians—is also present in Irenaeus.

The idea of the *sacrifice of Christ* is usually only implicit in his writing, but there is no question that it pervades his thought. It is presumed in several of the eucharistic texts (e.g., *Adv. Haer.* IV 29:5) and implied in two texts on the Passover and in another which speaks of Christ as high priest (*Adv. Haer.* IV 20:1; *Proof* 25; *Adv. Haer.* IV 16). It is also clearly presumed in his treatment of several central christological themes: the Servant theme (*Adv. Haer.* III 17:9; IV 37:2; *Proof* 68–69), the idea of the necessity of Christ's suffering (*Adv. Haer.* III 17:5 and 19:4), the ideas of sin offering (*Adv. Haer.* III 19:3 and 34) and redemption by blood (*Adv. Haer.* III 17:9), and the *hyper*-theme, that is, that Christ died *for* us (*Adv. Haer.* III 17:9 and 19:3).

But the central theme of Christ's sacrifice comes through strongest perhaps in a singular passage which can be characterized as summing up Irenaeus' Christology and soteriology. This passage portrays the physically real sacrifice of Christ as the very purpose of the incarnation. The word became flesh in order to be able to offer himself bodily in sacrifice and thereby save us:

> Thus he united man with God and brought about a communion between them, for we would otherwise have been unable to share in incorruptibility if he had not come to us. For incorruptibility, invisible and imperceptible as it is, would be no help to us; so he became visible that we might be taken up into full communion with incorruptibility. Because we are all connected with the first formation of Adam and were bound to death through disobedience, it was just and necessary that the bonds of death be loosed by him who was made man for us. Because death had established its dominion over the body, it was just and necessary that man who was once defeated by the body, should henceforth be free of its oppression. Thus, *the Word was made flesh* in order that sin, destroyed by means of the same flesh through which it

6. Justin in *1 Apol.* 32:1.5–9; *Trypho* 52:2; 53:1; 54:1–2; 63:2–3; 76:2. Irenaeus in *Adv. Haer.* IV 20:2 and *Proof* 57.

had gained its mastery and dominion, should no longer live in us. Thus did our Lord take up the same first formation [as Adam] in his incarnation, in order that he might offer it up in his struggle on behalf of his forefathers, and thus overcome through Adam what had stricken us through Adam.[7]

Behind this passage, of course, are Irenaeus' well-known theories of "recapitulation" and "exchange," that is, that Christ brought us together *under one head*, and that he did so by exchanging natures with us:

> That Word has at the end of time . . . united himself with his creation and become a mortal man. . . . And by becoming man, he restored anew the lengthy series of men in himself and brought them under one head (*recapitulavit*), and in short has given us salvation. Thus we regain in Christ Jesus what we had lost in Adam, namely, existence according to God's image and likeness. (*Adv. Haer.* III 18:1)

> The Word of God, our Lord Jesus Christ, because of his boundless love became what we are in order to make us what he is. (*Adv. Haer.* V Preface; cf. also III 19:1)

It is not difficult to recognize here what the later Fathers will call "divinization" or "deification" (cf. Smulders, *The Fathers on Christology*, 11–19), although the word itself is not used.

The *temple theme* is given a prominent place. *Adv. Haer.* V 6:2, Irenaeus' most extensive treatment of it, expands, as one would expect, upon the principal Pauline texts (1 Cor 3:16–17; 6:13–15). But Irenaeus also brings in the Johannine version of the temple logion ("destroy this temple . . . ," i.e., "of his body"— John 2:19, 21) to emphasize that our body is the temple not merely of God but also of Christ. Interestingly, Irenaeus seems to have picked up from Paul only the idea of the individual, but not that of the community, as the new temple. In any case, however, there is throughout a strong sense of concrete, physical realism, doubtless due to Irenaeus' anti-Gnostic concern. This concern helps us, in other passages, to understand his emphasis on a realistic understanding of Christ's presence in the Eucharist.

---

7. Proof of the Apostolic Preaching 31, translated from *Patrologia Orientalis* 12/5 (Paris: Firmin-Didot, 1919) 683 and 771.

He writes:

> How can they say that the flesh, which is nourished with the body
> of the Lord and with his blood, goes to corruption, and does not
> partake of life? . . . But our opinion is in accordance with the
> Eucharist, and the Eucharist in turn establishes our opinion.
> (*Adv. Haer.* IV 31:3)

Irenaeus also joins to the temple theme the ideas of universal
priesthood and of continual sacrifice. He points out how Jesus
(cf. Luke 6:1–5 parr) defends his disciples for plucking grain on
the sabbath by arguing that they too are priests and are, equiva-
lently, in the temple continually serving the Lord:

> . . . justifying his disciples by appealing to the law, and pointing
> out that it was lawful for the priests to work freely. For God
> appointed David a priest, although Saul had persecuted him. For
> all the just possess the sacerdotal rank. And all the apostles of
> the Lord are priests; they inherit here neither lands nor houses,
> but serve God and the altar continually. . . . The priests in the
> temple profaned the sabbath and were blameless. Why were
> they blameless? Because when in the temple they were not en-
> gaged in secular affairs, but in the service of the Lord. (*Adv.
> Haer.* IV 17)[8]

Thus we see how Irenaeus, in a way not open to Justin because
of his anti-Jewish polemic, has given a further development to
the dominical argument which implicitly made the Levitical
priesthood a partial model for the Christian priesthood.

When we move on to ask how Irenaeus understands the *sacrifice of the Christian,* we must turn to his extensive discussion of
sacrifice in *Adv. Haer.* IV 29:1–32. This is the most extensive

8. A little further on in *Adv. Haer.* IV 17 we find what appears to be
the only text which suggests that Irenaeus may have thought of the community and not just the individual as the Christian temple. The Proof of
the Apostolic Preaching 96 suggests, although he apparently gave little
thought to it, that he may also have been open to the idea of the whole
of Christian life as sacrificial: "There will be no command to remain idle
one day of rest to him who is always a keeper of the sabbath, who is in the
temple of God, which is the human body, serving God and at all times
working righteousness. For he says: 'I will have mercy and not sacrifice,
and knowledge of God more than burnt offerings'" (Hos 6:6; cf. Matt
12:7).

treatment of sacrifice from any second century Christian source. It could practically stand by itself as a short treatise in its own right. After discussing the need for the proper internal dispositions, he goes on to speak of the *"new oblation of the new covenant"*:

> But when he was instructing his disciples to offer to God the first-fruits of his creatures, not as if God needed this but that they themselves might be neither unfruitful nor ungrateful, he took that created thing, bread, and gave thanks, saying: "This is my body." And likewise the cup, which is part of that creation to which we belong, he confessed to be his blood, and taught the new oblation of the new covenant. This is what the church, receiving from the apostles, offers to God throughout the whole world, to him who gives for our subsistence the first fruits of his own gifts in the New Testament. This is what Malachi, one of the twelve prophets, thus foretold: "I have no pleasure in you, says the Lord almighty, and I will not accept sacrifice at your hands. For from the rising of the sun unto its setting my name is glorified among the nations, and in every place incense is offered to my name, and a pure sacrifice; for my name is great among the nations, says the Lord Almighty" [Mal 1:10–12]. By this he indicates in the plainest manner that the former people shall indeed cease to make offerings to God, but that in every place sacrifice— indeed pure sacrifice—will be offered to him, and that his name will be glorified among the nations. (*Adv. Haer.* IV 29:5)

Without doubt, then, the Eucharist is the sacrifice now offered by Christians throughout the world. But once again, what does this mean? All the evidence suggests that the eucharistic sacrifice is, as it was for Justin, the spiritualized one of prayers of praise and thanksgiving.

Irenaeus also clearly speaks of other things as sacrifices, for example, prayer in general (*Adv. Haer.* IV 30:1); and when he goes on to speak of "the offering of the church—*ecclesiae oblatio*" (IV 31:1), he leaves open, with typical vagueness, the basic question (in our minds) as to whether this offering includes or excludes the Eucharist. However, the continuation of this passage in IV 31:2–3 gives the very strong impression that he is thinking of many different kinds of offerings and not just of the

Eucharist.[9] There are many questions the modern theologian
would like to put to Irenaeus, but we must refrain from attempting to wring from him answers to questions which, in his time,
had not yet arisen.

Before leaving Irenaeus we must call particular attention to two
theologically significant developments. The first concerns the
relationship between incarnation and sacrifice. For, as we have
just indicated in discussing his idea of the sacrifice of Christ (pp.
93–94), Irenaeus presents the sacrifice of Christ as the very purpose of the incarnation.

The second development concerns the purpose of sacrifice. He
follows the tradition which sees atonement as the general purpose of sacrifice. But a number of passages, unfortunately available only in Latin translations, present the idea of sacrifice as
propitiatory (i.e., as a human action designed to have an effect
on God). He speaks of Jesus "propitiating God for men." Further on he rejects the idea of sinners "imagining that God was to
be propitiated"; but he follows this soon after by speaking of the
true sacrifice "by offering which they shall appease God."[10]
Other texts (e.g., IV 31:2) deny that God is appeased by sacrifice.

Although the evidence is not wholly consistent and we have
only Latin translations to work from, it is clear that some of
these texts appear to present man as the agent and God as the
object of an action called propitiation. However, since Irenaeus
is in general quite cognizant and respectful of the divine transcendence, it does not seem fair to assume on this evidence alone
that he thinks favorably of propitiation in the sense of a creature
presuming or hoping to exercise some control over God. But
whatever the case might be, it seems that these Latin phrases
contributed mightily to the establishment in Western Christian

9. The idea of the conscience of the offerer sanctifying the sacrifice
when it is pure (*Adv. Haer.* IV 31:2) can hardly refer to the Eucharist
alone. Also the reference to the test of suffering by which one is made
"acceptable" to God and the use of Phil 4:18 (*Adv. Haer.* IV 31:3)
reflect Paul's idea of the life and activity of the Christian as sacrificial.
But Irenaeus nowhere presents this with Paul's clarity and directness.

10. The operative Latin Phrases are: *"propitians pro hominibus Deum"*
(*Adv. Haer.* IV 16); *"putantes propitiari Deum"* (*Adv. Haer.* IV 29:1);
"quod offerentes propitiabuntur Deum" (*Adv. Haer.* IV 29:2).

thought of at least the language, if not also the idea, of propitiation.[11]

HIPPOLYTUS OF ROME

Unlike Justin and Irenaeus, Hippolytus, writing in the early third century, has a concept of sacrifice which is a bit more free of polemical preoccupations. He has an intensely realistic, physical conception of the self-offering of the word incarnate. So strong is the connection between incarnation and sacrifice that we can call it the *leitmotif* of Hippolytus' theology of sacrifice. This finds its strongest expression in a homily against the heresy of Noetus:

> I am not the one who says this, but he who has come down from heaven attests it; for he says: "no one has ascended into heaven but he who descended from heaven, the Son of man who is in heaven" (John 3:13). What then can he seek except what is proclaimed? Will he say that flesh was not in heaven? Yet there is the flesh which was presented by the word of the Father as an offering, the flesh that came from the Spirit and the Virgin and was shown to be the perfect Son of God. It is evident, therefore, that he offered himself to the Father. Before this there was no flesh in heaven. Who then was in heaven but the word incarnate who was sent to show that he was both on earth and also in heaven?[12]

As is obvious from the above passage, Hippolytus is very much at home with the idea of the sacrifice of Christ. We are not surprised to find him continuing the Christian tradition of seeing Christ as the only true Passover.[13]

11. One thinks of those Christians who feel that there is need to placate the divine anger or to repair the injury done to God by sin. This is not far from the Anselmian notion of atonement.

12. Against Noetus 4. Translated from E. Schwartz, *Zwei Predigten Hippolyts* (Sitzungsberichte der Bayerischen Akademie der Wissenshaften 3; 1936), 8. (For a full English translation cf. Ante Nicene Fathers V 223–31). The Refutation of All Heresies X 33:17 (GCS 26 [III] 291:29–292:5 and ANF V 152) is a sacrifice text equally explicit in its incarnational realism.

13. Refutation of All Heresies VIII 1. See also Apostolic Tradition 41 (see note 14 below; *ATC* 62) where the Old Testament bread of proposition is seen as a type of the body and blood of Christ, and the sacrificial lamb is seen as a type of the perfect lamb.

By Hippolytus' time, the gift theory of sacrifice, purified of all notions of divine need, had become a central pillar in the Christian theology of sacrifice. We can see this at work in the prayer of the bishop as he accepts the newly harvested first fruits (from the Coptic text of the Apostolic Tradition):[14] "We thank you, Lord God, and offer you the first fruits which you have given us, so that we might receive from them, since you brought them to fruition by your Word and commanded the earth to bring forth all fruits for the use, the enjoyment and the nourishment of the human race and of all creatures."[15]

However, Hippolytus is most known for what he has to say about the eucharistic sacrifice and priesthood in the Apostolic Tradition. Here he uses the word "offering" or "oblation" (*prosphora*) to signify both the eucharistic rite as a whole as well as the material offerings themselves. As in 1 Clement (see above, p. 86) it seems to have been the specific function of the bishop to receive the offerings and recite the eucharistic prayer over them (cf. *AT* 21; also 4 and 23 and *ATC* 47).

The concept of priesthood (implicitly perhaps also that of universal priesthood) is also present where Hippolytus speaks of those who have confessed the name of the Lord:

Hands are not to be laid on him for the office of deacon or that of a priest for he has (already) the dignity of the priesthood because of his confession. But if he is to be installed as bishop, then hands are to be laid on him. (*ATC* 34; cf. also *AT* 9 and 10)

We cannot assume that this "dignity of the priesthood" means priesthood in the full sense, for Hippolytus seems to reserve to the bishop alone the privilege of performing or presiding over the full eucharistic rite, and the bishop alone is described as having a high-priestly function, as making atonement, as having the power

14. The Apostolic Tradition, except for a few fragments from the original Greek, survives only in this Coptic version (*ATC*) edited by W. Till and J. Leipoldt, *Der Koptische Text der Kirchenordnung Hippolyts* (TU 58/3; Berlin: Akademie-Verlag, 1954). There is a different Latin version (*AT*) edited by B. Botte, *La Tradition Apostolique de Saint Hippolyte* (Liturgiegeschichtliche Quellen und Forschungen; Münster: Aschendorff, 1963).

15. *ATC* 53, p. 29.

to forgive sins, making an offering directly to God. The key text is from the rite of consecration for a bishop:

> Grant, you who know all hearts, unto this your servant whom you have chosen for the episcopacy, to feed your holy flock and to minister to you, without blemish, unceasingly, night and day, with high-priestly service to make atonement before you and to offer you the gifts of your holy church, and with the high-priestly spirit to have the power to forgive sins according to your commandment; to dispense the (ecclesiastical) offices according to your decree, to loose every bond in accordance with the power which you gave the apostles, to be pleasing to you in mildness and purity of heart, offering to you an odor of sweetness through your Son Jesus Christ our Lord, with whom be glory and power and honor to you, with the Holy Spirit, now and forever and unto all ages. Amen. (AT 3)

Thus it is that Hippolytus does not merely continue the tradition of looking upon Christ as the Christian Passover, nor simply develop further the growing tradition which sees the Eucharist as sacrifice. He combines, especially in Against Noetus 4, his incarnational Christology and soteriology with the gift idea of sacrifice in such a way as to produce a new moment in the development of the Christian idea of sacrifice. Briefly stated: the eternal word of God became man in order to be able to rise again to heaven and there offer to the eternal Father not only his flesh, his manhood, but also man himself. This offering to the Father, implying a theme of divinization, enables us also to share what the Father has granted his Son. This exciting theological development, however, is unfortunately given no direct treatment in the Apostolic Tradition. We are consequently left with no discussion of the relation between the theology and the ritual (i.e., eucharistic liturgy) of sacrifice.

TWO SECOND CENTURY TREATISES ON THE PASSOVER

The Peri Pascha (PP—On the Passover) of Melito of Sardis,[16] and the anonymous, apparently Quartodeciman In S. Pascha (IP

16. O. Perler, *Méliton de Sardes sur la Pâque* (SC 123; Paris: Cerf, 1966). The date (A.D. 160–170) and authenticity of this work is well established.

—On the Holy Passover),[17] represent a genre of basically liturgical or homiletic compositions which give a specifically Christian development to the Jewish Passover haggadah on Exodus 12. Two themes are particularly relevant to our study: 1) the Eucharist and Passion of Christ as the Christian Passover, 2) the "spiritual Passover."

In these writings, the Passover, the Passion of Jesus Christ, and the Eucharist are, for all practical purposes, identified. "The lamb is immolated toward evening. For it is indeed at the setting of the sun that the sacred Lamb of God is put to death" (*IP* 23). "The flesh [of the Passover lamb] is eaten at night, for the light of the world has set upon the great body of Christ: 'Take, eat, this is my body'" (*IP* 26; cf. *PP* 2-3). Some of the theological richness that we have just seen in Hippolytus is also detectable here:

> This was the Pasch which Jesus desired to suffer for us [cf. Luke 22:15]; by suffering he freed us from suffering, and by death he conquered death, and through the visible food he won for us his immortal life. This was the saving desire of Jesus, this his totally spiritual love, to prove the types to be types, and, in their place, to give his sacred body to his disciples: "Take, eat, this is my body; take, drink, this is my blood, the new covenant, which is to be shed for many for the forgiveness of sins." For this reason his desire to eat was not as great as his desire to suffer, in order to free us from the suffering incurred by eating.[18]

From earliest Christianity (cf. Rom 12:1; 1 Pet 2:5) the Greek adjective *logikos* ("spiritual" or "reasonable") was often used to describe that worship or sacrifice which is Christian. These two treatises provide precious insights into the specifically Christian content of this concept. "In order that we might be fully

---

17. P. Nautin, *Homélies Paschales I: Une Homélie Inspiree du Traite sur la Pâque d'Hippolyte* (SC 27; Paris: Cerf, 1950). R. Cantalamessa, *L'Omelia "In S. Pascha" dello Pseudo-Ippolito di Roma* (Milan: 1967), appears to have fairly well demonstrated the Quartodeciman (second century Jewish-Christian communities in Asia Minor) origins of this work and its close kinship with Melito's treatise.

18. *IP* 49.

fed by the Word (*logos*)," we are exhorted, "not with earthly but with heavenly nourishment, let us also eat the Passover of the Word [or spiritual Passover—*to logikon pascha*] with that spiritual desire with which the Lord himself desired to eat it with us when he said: [Luke 22:15] 'with desire have I desired to eat this Pasch with you'" (*IP* 4).

Clearly, we have to do not with just a "spiritual Passover," but quite specifically with "the Lord's Passover." So throughout these treatises (*IP* 27; *PP* 3; 4; 6; 7; 9) the words *logos* and *logikos* refer specifically to the divine Logos who became man. The meaning is overwhelmingly christological. Thus, to translate *logikos* as "reasonable" or even "spiritual" may be misleading as well as inadequate. For *logikos*, in the early Christian context, seems to signify first and foremost "of Christ" or simply "Christian."

THE SECOND CENTURY ACTS OF THE MARTYRS

The idea of martyrdom as sacrifice develops naturally, one might say, from seeing first Christ's death as sacrificial and then Christian life as an imitation of Christ. We have seen how intertestamental Judaism looked upon the death of the Maccabean martyrs as sacrificial (above, p. 34), and how Ignatius of Antioch looked forward to his own martyrdom as a sacrificial offering (above, pp. 86–87). The same idea permeates the seven Acts of the Martyrs which come from all over the empire in the last half of the second century. The use of sacrificial imagery is sometimes quite extensive:

> And he, with his hands bound behind him, like a choice ram taken from a great flock for sacrifice, an acceptable whole burnt offering prepared for God, looked up to heaven and said: ". . . I bless you for making me worthy of this day and hour, that I should take part among the numbers of the martyrs in the cup of your Christ . . . among whom may I be accepted before you today as a rich and acceptable sacrifice." (*Mart. Pol.* 14:1–2)

The martyr's constancy is sometimes described in terms reminiscent of the Stoic hero's *apatheia* (supremacy of reason over the passions). However, this theme is only marginal. For the real cause of the Christian martyr's constancy is a Christ-mysticism, that is, the Christian in the act of martyrdom, being taken up into unity with Jesus Christ. The fellow martyrs of Blandina, exposed to the beasts, "during the contest, even with the eyes of the flesh, saw in the person of their sister him who was crucified for them" (Letter of the Churches of Vienne and Lyons 41). Felicitas, in the pains of childbirth shortly before her own martyrdom, affirms: "Now I suffer what I suffer: but then another will be in me who will suffer for me, because I too am to suffer for Him" (Passion of SS. Perpetua and Felicitas 15:3). Not surprisingly, then, allusions to a Suffering Servant Christology are also found in this literature.[19]

In these writings, apparently inspired by the same image in the New Testament epistles (1 Cor 9:25-27; Phil 3:14; Jude 3; Heb 12:1; 1 Tim 1:18; 6:12-13; 2 Tim 4:6-8), martyrdom is also seen as an athletic or gladiatorial combat. There are two main aspects of this view: first, the devil, not the beasts or executioners, is the adversary (cf. Perpetua and Felicitas 10; Vienne and Lyons 5-6); second, martyrdom is sometimes seen as the martyr's own personal achievement. The clearest and most extreme example is the attitude of Saturninus: "Whenever they talked among themselves about their hopes for martyrdom, Saturninus declared that he wished to be cast to all the beasts so indeed would he wear a more glorious crown" (Perpetua and Felicitas 19:1-2). We see here not only the beginnings of that imprudent rushing into martyrdom about which Clement of Alexandria complained, but also the beginnings of a tendency toward Pelagian attitudes and overly enthusiastic hagiographical embellishment. In their second century context, however, these tendencies were still reasonably subordinate to the narrator's primary purpose of emphasizing union with God as the source of the martyr's strength.

The idea of *spiritual sacrifice* is also found in these accounts in a way that would do full justice to the concerns of Justin and Athenagoras, as we can see from Apollonius' defense:

19. See especially Martyrdom of S. Polycarp 14:1 and Letter of the Churches of Vienne and Lyons 23.

It was my hope, proconsul, that these religious discussions would help you and that the eyes of your soul would have been illumined by my defense, so that your heart would bear fruit and worship God the maker of all; and that to him alone, day by day and by means of almsgiving and brotherly love, you would offer your prayers, an unbloody and pure sacrifice to God. (Acts of Apollonius 44; see also 8)

Thus Apollonius defends a concept of Christian sacrifice which seems to be realized not in cultic worship but in the practical living of the Christian life. We cannot presume to conclude from so few texts that this exhausts the idea of sacrifice held by Apollonius or the authors of these works. But since it is the one view they do mention, we can only conclude that it was very important to them.

THE ALEXANDRIAN TRADITION: PHILO, BARNABAS, CLEMENT OF ALEXANDRIA, AND ORIGEN

Alexandria was the second Athens of the ancient world. This was where, in the third and second centuries B.C., the Hebrew Scriptures were first translated into Greek. It was where Philo, the great Jewish religious philosopher, flourished contemporaneously with St. Paul and produced a body of literature which, after the Scriptures, had an influence on later Christian thought unequaled by anything of its time. It was also the home of Clement and Origen, theological giants who, in that late second and early third century A.D., were equaled perhaps only by Tertullian. The rich theology of sacrifice developed by these Alexandrians is sufficiently unique to require the separate treatment we now accord it.

Philo of Alexandria

Philo of Alexandria represents the high point of the flourishing Jewish-Hellenistic, philosophico-religious "school" which systematically attempted to reshape the philosophy of the Greeks according to the pattern of a completely different (i.e., Jewish) faith. Philo's writings, for example, are permeated with Platonic and Stoic views. But whenever he begins to speak of the nature of God, or of our relation to God, Greek philosophy gives way almost completely to Hebrew faith. He does not write systematically of sacrifice in any one place. But, from the hundreds of passages in which he mentions or treats of sacrifice, it is possible to sketch out a highly developed theology of sacrifice which in early antiquity was surpassed in richness and depth only by Origen, and in influence on Christian theology perhaps only by the Scriptures themselves.

The Alexandrian Jews had developed an *allegorical method* for interpreting Scripture. Philo thus believed that a passage could either 1) be literally true or 2) be literally true but also have an allegorical meaning, or 3) be true only in an allegorical sense, or 4) be doubtful in its literal sense but certain in its allegorical meaning. His own overriding intent in reading and interpreting Scripture was to write an allegorical account of the human soul in its progress toward God. Thus he looked not just for "the meaning of the words" but also for "the deeper meaning," as we can see in his interpretation of Noah's sacrifice in Gen 8:20:

> *This is the literal meaning. But as for the deeper meaning,* the clean beasts and birds are the senses and the mind of the wise man, (for) in the mind the thoughts rove about. And it is proper to bring all these, when they have altogether become fruits, as a thank-offering to the Father, and to offer them as immaculate and unblemished offerings for sacrifices.[20]

When Philo analyzes the idea of sacrifice, he uses the familiar philosophical and prophetic criticisms of the cult. Most central, however, is not philosophy but religion, more precisely his faith in God as Creator and Lord of all. It is from this belief that he develops his favorite moral on the subject of sacrifice: *we can only give to God what God has first given us*—"Whatsoever you bring as an offering, you will offer God's possessions and not your own" (On the Sacrifices of Cain and Abel 97). This particular view of

20. Philo, Questions and Answers on Genesis II 52. The translations of Philo are those of F. H. Colson, G. H. Whitaker, R. Marcus, and J. W. Earp in the Loeb Classical Library edition (Cambridge: Harvard University, 1958–62).

the gift theory of sacrifice soon became an important part of the Christian idea of sacrifice.

More particularly, Philo's idea of sacrifice can be studied under the general heading of an *allegory of the soul's progress toward God*. Under this we can distinguish seven headings: 1) the Passover as a symbol of the soul's progress; 2) true sacrifice as an offering of the whole self—the soul, the mind, and the heart; 3) the acceptance of sacrifice and the primacy of dispositions; 4) the purpose of sacrifice; 5) the high priest; 6) the idea of universal priesthood; 7) the temple, sanctuary, and altar.

1) *The Passover is a symbol of the soul's progress.* Since Philo sees human life itself as essentially a progress or passing over from the material to the spiritual, he not surprisingly sees in the historic Israelite "passing over" from bondage to freedom a ready-made symbol of the soul's progress toward God. The soul makes the Passover sacrifice when it begins to give up the pursuits and disorders of youth, when the mind changes from ignorance and stupidity to education and wisdom, etc.[21]

2) *True sacrifice is an offering of the whole self—the soul, the mind, and the heart.* "The true oblation, what else can it be but the devotion of a soul which is dear to God?" (Moses II 108). At times Philo looks beyond this to see life itself as sacrificial: "Sacrifice is not flesh but the pure and unstained life of a holy person."[22] This reminds us of the New Testament texts which speak of the Christian life as sacrificial. But there is one great difference: the New Testament is consciously incarnational, while Philo has a typically Platonic bias against matter.

3) *The acceptance of sacrifice and the primacy of dispositions* becomes increasingly important for Philo as he shifts attention from the ritual itself to the spiritual meaning (cf., among numerous others, On the Special Laws I 167).

21. Philo, Questions and Answers on Exodus I 4; cf. also Allegorical Interpretation III 94; On the Sacrifices of Abel and Cain 51 and 63; Questions and Answers on Exodus I 3; 11; 12; 15; 19; On the Preliminary Studies 105–6.

22. Questions and Answers on Exodus II 98; cf. also On the Special Laws (*de Specialibus Legibus*) I 272.

4) *The purpose of sacrifice* is, first, to honor God and, second, to benefit the worshiper. The latter has the positive function of obtaining blessings and the negative function of obtaining release from evil. There is also in Philo, distinguishing him from most of rabbinic Judaism, a strong emphasis on the "Gnostic intention" which sees the purpose, for example, of sin offerings, more in education than in atonement, and sees atonement itself primarily as an affair of the *mind*, that is, purification is first and foremost a matter of knowledge, especially self-knowledge.[23]

5) *The high priest.* Philo oscillates between a Jewish idealization and Hellenistic spiritualization of the idea of priesthood. The spiritualizing influence is particularly strong in his idea of the high priest whom he raises to a more than human level. As we would expect, he speaks of the divine word *(logos theios)* in exalted terms: "Image of God, chiefest of all beings intellectually perceived, placed nearest with no intervening distance to the Alone truly existent One" (On Flight and Finding 101). But he also applies the same exalted language to the high priest, practically equating him with the Logos: "We say, then, that the high priest is not a man but a divine word and immune from all unrighteousness whether intentional or unintentional" (On Flight and Finding 109; see also On the Special Laws I 116). This view forms an essential part of the background of at least the language and imagery of the Christian Alexandrians in their theology of Christ, the Divine Logos, High Priest, and Mediator.

Philo's allegorical interpretation of the high priest's garments, a theme also quite common in other Jewish literature of the period, becomes a means of expressing his teaching on universal salvation. For these garments express the wish that the high priest, by constantly contemplating the "image of the all" upon his own person, should make "his own life worthy of the sum of things." These garments also express the wish that, in performing his office, he have the whole universe as his fellow ministrant. Finally, they also indicate that he is to pray and give thanks not

23. Cf. On the Special Laws I 191–93; 202–4; 262–66; Questions and Answers on Genesis III 3; Moses II 97; On Dreams I 209–12.

only on behalf of the whole human race but also for the rest of creation.[24]

6) *The idea of universal priesthood* is one of the pillars of Philo's theology. He associates it particularly with the Passover when, in the beginning, the whole nation carried out the priestly functions in harmony.[25] But most significant of all are the several texts which insist that it is basically ethical purity which confers priesthood. For example, "He [Moses] encourages those who no longer tread the path of wrongdoing with the thought that their resolution to purify themselves has given them a place in the sacerdotal cast and advanced them to equal honor with the priest."[26]

7) *The temple, sanctuary, and altar* are realities around which Philo tended to center his most characteristic statements on the theology of sacrifice. With the word temple, Philo would be thinking, to some extent, of the actual temple or city of Jerusalem, a bit more extensively of the whole world or universe as God's temple, but most extensively and primarily of the rational soul or mind of the wise person as God's temple.

In ascending order of importance, the Jerusalem temple is valued primarily for the spiritual meaning behind it, although the extensive attention it receives shows that Philo is not indifferent to its physical reality. In the true sense, however, only the universe and the rational soul are temples; and the former of these, the universe as temple, inevitably involves the far more important idea of the rational soul or mind as temple:

> There are, as is evident, two temples of God: one of them this universe, in which there is also as high priest his First-born, the

24. On the Special Laws I 84–97; cf. also Moses II 109–35; Questions and Answers on Exodus II 107–24; On Flight and Finding 110; On Dreams I 215. Other Jewish literature: Wisdom of Solomon 18:24; Testament of Levi 8:2; Josephus' *Antiquities* III 151–87. Philo's universalism is also expressed elsewhere, notably in his detailed exposition of the sacrificial code: On the Special Laws I 168–90).

25. Questions and Answers on Exodus I 10. See also On the Special Laws I 70; 145; 249; Moses II 224–25; On the Decalogue 159; On Abraham 198; On the Contemplative Life 74.

26. On the Special Laws I 243; cf. also II 163; 164; On Drunkenness 126.

divine Word, and the other the rational soul, whose priest is the
real man; the outward and visible image of whom is he who
offers the prayers and sacrifices handed down from our fathers,
to whom it has been committed to wear the aforesaid tunic.[27]

Philo's understanding of the soul as temple is consistent with
his theological anthropology which insisted that not man's body
but only his soul is created in God's image and likeness, and that
therefore only the spiritual part of man can come close enough
to the divine to become God's temple (On the Creation 69). The
contrast with the Pauline and incarnational, Christian views on
the body is striking.

The idea of the soul-temple as God's dwelling place is clearly
present: "For what more worthy house could be found for God
throughout the whole world of creation, than a soul . . . ?" (On
Sobriety 62). Nevertheless, Philo is not talking about what we
would understand as "divine indwelling." For the dynamic involved is not that of God "coming down" to live in our soul or
mind, but rather that of a Gnostic-like elevation of the soul or
mind to the contemplation of things divine.[28]

This puts in context what Philo has to say about the soul-
temple as the true place of worship:

> The true altar of God is the thankful soul of the Sage, compacted
> of perfect virtues unsevered and undivided, for no part of virtue
> is useless. On this soul-altar the sacred light is ever burning
> and carefully kept unextinguished, and the light of the mind is
> wisdom, just as the darkness of the soul is folly. For knowledge
> is to the reason what the light of the senses is to the eye: as that
> gives the apprehension of material things, so does knowledge
> lead to the contemplation of things immaterial and conceptual,
> and its beam shines for ever, never dimmed nor quenched. (On
> the Special Laws I 287–88)

Thus we see that Philo's idea of the soul-temple as the place
of worship centers in the altar. But it is not the incense-altar, as
his notion of its sublime superiority would lead us to expect; for

---

27. On Dreams I 215. Cf. also On Noah's Work as a Planter 50; Who
Is the Heir? 75.
28. Cf. also On Sobriety 63–64; Questions and Answers on Exodus II 51.

the continually burning sacred fire and the allusion to the unhewn stones (Exod 20:25) refer specifically to the altar of burnt sacrifice which Philo otherwise thinks very little of. On this point at least, Philo did not bring image and idea into full harmony. However, what he is saying is fairly clear. The idea of the soul as God's temple stands in the service of his ethics. But ethics or the ethical life is not the goal; it is merely a preparation for mystical experience or mystical contemplation: "the contemplation of things immaterial and conceptual."

Once again, the similarity and contrast with Christian thought are illuminating. Origen, as we shall see, is indebted to Philo (or the tradition represented by Philo) for the imagery of the soul as altar on which there burns continually the fire of divine worship. But where Philo saw ethics as merely the propaedeutic to this worship conceived of in terms of a nonmaterial contemplation of (Platonic) verities, Origen and the Christians, for all their propensity toward the glory of mystical contemplation, usually did not lose sight of the fact that Christian worship essentially involves the ethical—that it is realized not so much in contemplation as in the living of an incarnationally inspired life of service.

Barnabas

The tract called the Epistle of Barnabas (ca. A.D. 130) is fiercely anti-Jewish. But through its polemical ardor shine some of the foundational insights of the early Christian theology of sacrifice. It exercised an influence far greater than its current modest reputation would suggest, for even as late as Origen's time it was often considered to be part of the inspired Scriptures.

In his allegorical interpretation of Scripture, the author of this tract owes much to the Philonic tradition. However, his basic principle of interpretation is radically different: he sees everything in Scripture (i.e., Old Testament) as pointing, in its only true sense, the spiritual sense, solely to the revelation of Jesus Christ who came in the flesh to save us. Thus he is even more radically allegorical than Philo, for he completely rejects literal interpretation as the typical Jewish error caused by the misleading influence of "an evil angel" (*Barn.* 9:5). We rightly criticize him for eliminating the role of the Old Testament from salvation-history. Some have also accused him of docetism (the theory that Jesus only *seemed* to be human); but that charge is clearly refuted by one of the most directly stated and repeatedly emphasized aspects of Barnabas' teaching: the physical reality of Christ's incarnation.

Barnabas' criticism of the cult, unlike that of other authors, is of a wholly religious nature and is directed solely against Old Testament sacrifice. He takes the classical texts of Old Testament cult criticism (Isa 1:11–13; Jer 7:22–23; Ps 51:19; Zech 8:17) and interprets them in a narrowly literal way (showing that he is willing to interpret Scripture literally when it suits his purpose) in order to reject Old Testament sacrifice entirely. He will accept only the spiritualized sacrifice of the Christian church, something that is "not made by man" (*Barn.* 2:6), implying that everything else is of human invention and thus infected with idolatry.

Expressed more positively, the central core of Barnabas' theology of sacrifice is his faith in the incarnation. He sees Jesus as the Son of God, preexistent and working with the Father at the creation, and who truly became flesh for us. He uses the word "flesh" (*sarx*) to describe Christ's incarnation no less than twelve times in this relatively brief work.[29] Finally, Christ's Passion and death are seen as sacrificial in a variety of ways, especially by intensely christological interpretations: 1) of the fasting rules for the Day of Atonement, 2) of the priestly regulations for eating the flesh of the sin offering, 3) of the scapegoat ritual of the Day of Atonement, and 4) of the rite of the red heifer (Num 19) which was used to obtain the waters of purification (Barnabas 7 and 8).

When we come to the sacrificing activity of Christians themselves, we find that the theme of the *Christian as temple of God* is central. "Let us be spiritual (*pneumatikoi*), let us be a temple

---

29. Chap. 6, where, among other places, the theme of the Suffering Servant is also alluded to, has the greatest single concentration of these occurrences.

consecrated to God" (4:11) Barnabas exhorts. Nor is he just speaking of the mind or soul as Philo would: "The habitation of our hearts is a shrine holy to the Lord" (6:15). Or, in his own words:

> (6) But let us inquire if a temple of God exists. Yes, it exists, where he himself said that he makes and perfects it. For it is written, "And it shall come to pass when the week is ended that a temple of God shall be built gloriously in the name of the Lord" [cf. Dan 9:24–27]. (7) I find then that a temple exists. Learn then how it will be built in the name of the Lord. Before we believed in God, the habitation of our heart was corrupt and weak, like a temple really built with hands, because it was full of idolatry and was the house of demons through doing things which were contrary to God. (8) "But it shall be built in the name of the Lord" [cf. Dan 9:24–27]. Now give heed, so that the temple of the Lord may be built gloriously. Learn in what way. When we received the remission of sins, and put our hope in the name, we became new, being created again from the beginning [cf. Mark 10:6; Matt 19:4; Eph 2:15]; wherefore God truly dwells in us, in the habitation which we are. (9) How? His word of faith, the calling of his promise, the wisdom of the ordinances, the commands of the teaching, himself prophesying in us, himself dwelling in us, by opening the door of the temple (that is the mouth) to us, who have been enslaved to death, into the incorruptible temple. (10) For he who desires to be saved looks not at the man, but at him who dwells and speaks in him, and is amazed at him, for he has never either heard him speak such words with his mouth, nor has he himself ever desired to hear them. This is the spiritual temple being built for the Lord. (*Barn.* 16:6–10)

It is not the antimaterial, radically spiritualizing temple theology of Philo that is operative here, but the incarnational temple theology of Paul. Barnabas is quite close to 1 Pet 2:9–10 and Rom 15:16 in giving the temple theme a decidedly apostolic or kerygmatic interpretation. Beyond this, there may also be a literary relationship between 1 Pet 2:5 and *Barn.* 16:10.

Clement of Alexandria

Clement of Alexandria (A.D. 140/150 to 211/215) is the first great figure of the so-called Alexandrian school of Christian theology. He is Platonic in thought and so deeply indebted to Philo that one might call him a Christian Philo. He harmonizes what he found in his Alexandrian predecessors around his own central hermeneutical principle: the life and worship of the Christian Gnostic. But two major points separate him from Philo and his Gnostic contemporaries: 1) his faith in the incarnation and 2) his faith in the church as the mediator and guarantor of the true, saving gnosis. As we did with Philo and Barnabas, we will arrange the material according to both the central themes of our own study and the relative weight Clement seemed to give to them. This yields five main divisions: 1) the interpretation of Scripture, 2) cult criticism and the idea of spiritual sacrifice, 3) the sacrifice of Christ, 4) the sacrifice of the Christians, 5) the temple and the altar.

1) *Interpretation of Scripture.* He shares with orthodox Christianity his faith in the unity of the two testaments, and with the Alexandrians a love of the flamboyant allegorizing developed by Philo, baptized by Barnabas, and later perfected by Origen. More than any other Father, and quite differently from Irenaeus, he uses the noun *gnosis* to refer to the true, spiritual meaning of Scripture, and its adjectival and adverbial forms to describe the Christian life. For example:

> The sacrifice acceptable to God is unswerving abstraction from the body and its passions. This is the really true piety. Is not, then, Socrates correct in calling philosophy the practice of Death? . . . It was from Moses that the chief of the Greeks drew these philosophical tenets. For Moses commands holocausts to be skinned and divided into parts [cf. Lev. 1:6]. For the Gnostic soul must be consecrated to the light, stripped of the coverings of matter, separated from the frivolousness of the body and of all the passions which are acquired through vain and lying opinions, and divested of the lusts of the flesh. (Stromata V 11)

As usual with Clement, the allegory is not presented as the interpretation of *specific* scriptural texts; instead, a mere general allusion to Scripture suffices. In fact, Clement often seems to treat the Bible as a symbolic poem rather than as the object of careful exegesis.

2) *Cult criticism and the idea of spiritual sacrifice.* Clement

113

not only follows Philo in seeing Old Testament sacrifices as symbols of the soul's progress toward God, and Barnabas in rejecting the validity of a literal interpretation of these sacrifices; he also goes beyond this by using at some length the cult criticism of the pagan philosophers and poets and not continually referring to the authority of Scripture. The result is a Christian cult criticism whose distinctive and formative influence seems to have been the religious philosophy of Hellenistic Judaism and of Greek philosphy. The most characteristic examples of Clement's cult criticism are passages (like Stromata V 11–12; V 14; VII 5–6) which combine all three types: straight philosophical analysis, a mélange of Scripture texts, references to and quotations from the philosophers and poets. Clement's criticism also goes beyond the merely theoretical or negative to describe what the cult of the Christian or "true Gnostic" should be:

> We ought to offer God not costly sacrifices but such as he loves, and in that mixture of incense which is mentioned in the law. It consists of many tongues and voices in prayer [cf. Exod 30:34–36], or rather of different nations and natures, prepared by the gift promised in the dispensation for "the unity of the faith" [Eph 4:13], and brought together in praise, with a pure mind, and just and right conduct, from holy works and righteous prayer. (Stromata VII 6)

3) *The Sacrifice of Christ* is mentioned in a variety of ways: in speaking of Christ as a whole burnt offering for us, as the Passover, as the Suffering Servant and as Lamb of God (Stromata V 10–11; Paedagogus II 8 and elsewhere). Further, Clement's Isaac-Christ typology highlights the theological importance of his understanding of the sacrifice of Christ:

> Where, then, was the door by which the Lord showed himself? The flesh by which he was manifested. He is Isaac (for the narrative may be interpreted otherwise), who is a type of the Lord, a child as a son. For he was the son of Abraham, as Christ was the Son of God; and a sacrifice like the Lord, only he was not immolated as the Lord was. Isaac only bore the wood of the cross. And he laughed mystically, prophesying that the Lord would fill us with joy, who have been redeemed from corruption by the blood of the Lord. Isaac did everything

but suffer, as was right, yielding the precedence in suffering to the Word. Furthermore, there is an intimation of the divinity of the Lord in his not being slain. For Jesus rose again after his burial, having suffered no harm, like Isaac released from sacrifice. (Paedagogus I 5; cf. also Stromata II 5).

It is interesting to note how Clement both adopts and modifies the Jewish haggadah on the sacrifice of Isaac which we sketched above at the end of Chapter Three.

The *incarnation* provides the background and foundation of Clement's understanding of Christ's sacrifice. This is expressed not quite so forcefully as in Barnabas, but no less clearly:

For this also he came down. For this he clothed himself with man. For this he voluntarily subjected himself to the experiences of men, that by bringing himself to the measure of our weakness whom he loved, he might correspondingly bring us to the measure of his own strength. And about to be offered up and giving himself as ransom, he left for us a new covenant-testament: My love I give unto you.[30]

The figure of Christ the high priest provides the specific model for Clement's understanding of Christ's sacrifice. "High priest" can have three meanings for Clement: first, the Old Testament high priest; second, Jesus Christ, and third, the true Gnostic or Christian. The second meaning is, of course, the central one for Clement; but in his thought the christological meaning not only flows naturally from the Old Testament type, it also seems to merge, at times, into the third meaning where the true Gnostic also becomes a "high priest." This is most clearly seen at the end of a long passage in which he is making use of the Philonic allegory of the high priest's robe in the context of the Day of Atonement liturgy.

And he shall take off the linen robe, which he had put on when he entered into the holy place; and shall lay it aside there, and wash his body in water in the holy place, and put on his robe [Lev 16:23–24]. One way, I think, of taking off and putting on the robe takes place when the Lord descends into the region of sense. Another way takes place when he who through him has

30. Quis dives salvetur 37. See also Stromata I 21; V 6; Paedagogus I 6.

believed, takes off and puts on, as the apostle intimated, the consecrated stole [cf. Eph 6:13–17]. Thence, after the image of the Lord, the worthiest were chosen from the sacred tribes to be high priests. . . . (Stromata V 6)

We are not surprised, in this allegorizing Alexandrian context, that Clement sees the taking off and putting on of the high priest's robe as symbolizing the incarnation. But he then goes boldly beyond this to suggest that the Christian believer, precisely as believer, shares in Christ's high-priestly dignity. Clement then ends by metahistorically reversing the normal roles of type and antitype so that Christ incarnate—and in him the Christian believer or true Gnostic—becomes the true archetype of the Old Testament high priests.

Protrepticus 12 singles out two high-priestly functions of Jesus: the one, directed toward us, is the sanctifying activity of preparing us for the eucharistic meal; the other, directed toward God, is Christ's mediating or intercessory activity for us. Elsewhere Clement speaks more directly about the specifically sacrificial aspects of Jesus' high-priestly activity:

If then, we say that the Lord the great high priest offers to God the incense of sweet fragrance, let us not imagine that this is a sacrifice and sweet fragrance of incense but let us understand it to mean that the Lord lays the acceptable offering of love, the spiritual fragrance, on the altar. (Paedagogus II 8)

It is noteworthy that this passage, the only one we have found in Clement which directly describes the sacrificial activity of Christ the high priest, speaks mainly in the language of spiritual sacrifice. This is consistent with Clement's general tendency to minimize the human aspects of Christ's high priesthood. It also fits in with his tendency to minimize, at least in relation to most other early Christian writers, the negative (i.e., atoning or sin-forgiving) aspects of redemption (atonement) and sacrifice.

4) *The sacrifice of the Christian.* Clement faithfully develops the primitive Christian understanding of the relationship between the sacrifice of Christ and the sacrifice of the Christian: "We glorify him who gave himself in sacrifice for us, we also sacrificing

ourselves" (Stromata VII 3; cf. 1 John 3:16). Clement's ideas in this area can be arranged under three headings: 1) the worship of the Gnostic, 2) universal priesthood, and 3) Gnostic martyrdom.

The *worship of the Gnostic*, that is, the Gnostic's prayer and sacrifice, is equivalent to the life of the Gnostic or the Gnostic's spiritual progress toward God. Clement calls this *"Gnostic assimilation"*:

> This is the function of the Gnostic who has been made perfect to have converse with God through the great high priest, and who is being made like the Lord, as far as possible, in the whole service of God which tends to the salvation of men through its provident care for us as well as through service, teaching, and the active ministry. The Gnostic even forms and creates himself; and he also, like God, adorns those who hear him, assimilating as far as possible the moderation which, arising from practice, tends to impassibility. He has, especially, uninterrupted converse and fellowship with the Lord. Mildness, I think, and philanthropy, and eminent piety, are the rules of Gnostic assimilation. I affirm that these virtues "are a sacrifice acceptable in the sight of God" [cf. Phil 4:18]; Scripture alleging that "the humble heart with right knowledge is the holocaust of God" [cf. Ps 51:17, 19–LXX 50:19, 21], each man who is admitted to holiness being illuminated unto indissoluble union. (Stromata VII 3)

Clement fills out his theology of Christian sacrifice by pointing out that the Christian becomes, like Christ, the offering itself: "We have become a consecrated offering to God for Christ's sake" (Protrepticus 4). This Christian worship is also strongly communal: "Does he not also know the other kind of sacrifice which consists in the giving both of doctrine and of money to those who need?" (Stromata VII 7). What Clement calls the "sacrifice of the church" is conceived of as something intensely communal:

> Breathing together is properly said of the church. For the sacrifice of the church is the word breathing as incense from holy souls, the sacrifice and the whole mind being at the same time unveiled to God. . . . Thus we should offer God not costly sacrifices but such as he loves. The mixture of incense mentioned in the law is something that consists of many tongues and voices in prayer, or rather of different nations and natures, prepared by the

gift bestowed in the dispensation for "the unity of the faith" [Eph 4:13] and brought together in praises, with a pure mind, and just and right conduct, from holy works and righteous prayer. (Stromata VII 6)

The echoes of those New Testament passages which speak of Christian life as sacrificial come through clearly. We are also reminded how Irenaeus and Hippolytus spoke of the "offering of the church." But while they were speaking of the Eucharist as sacrificial, Clement may not have had the Eucharist in mind at all. For in these passages it is clear that he is looking at the whole life of the Gnostic as sacrificial worship, or, in his own words, as a "holding festival . . . in our whole life" (Stromata VII 7). His concept of sacrifice is thus thoroughly spiritualized, but by no means radically dematerialized.

Finally, we must look to Clement's lengthy description of the life of the Gnostic (in Stromata VII 11–16) in order to see how the worship of the Gnostic fits into its full context. There we see that the practical concerns of active life in the church and among men is as much a part of Clement's idea of the Christian life as is the actual worship and contemplation of the Gnostic. As Clement himself says: "The end of the Gnostic here is, in my judgment, twofold: partly scientific contemplation, partly action" (Stromata VII 16).

Universal priesthood is central for Clement, for the true Gnostic is "the truly kingly man; he is the sacred high priest of God" (Stromata IV 25). The following three paragraphs unfold this at length. They also contain Clement's only significant discussion of ecclesiastical office and of the relationship between the hierarchical priesthood and universal priesthood:

He, who has first moderated his passions and trained himself for impassibility and developed to the beneficence of Gnostic perfection, is here equal to the angels. Already luminous and shining like the sun in the exercise of beneficence, he speeds by righteous knowledge through the love of God to the sacred abode, just like the apostles. Now the apostles did not become such by being chosen for some distinguished quality of nature, since Judas also was chosen along with them. But they were capable of becoming apostles on being chosen by him who forsees even ultimate issues. Matthias, accordingly, who was not chosen along with them, on showing himself worthy of becoming an apostle, is substituted for Judas.

But now, those who have exercised themselves in the Lord's commandments, and lived perfectly and gnostically according to the gospel, may also be enrolled in the chosen body of the apostles. For what actually makes such a person a presbyter is not that he does and teaches the Lord's work because of being ordained by men, nor is it that he is considered to be righteous because he is a presbyter; but rather, such a person is enrolled in the presbyterate because he is righteous. And even though here on earth he should not be honored with the chief seat (cf. Mark 12:39 parr), he will sit down on the twenty-four thrones (Rev 4:4 11:16; cf. Matt 19:28 par), judging the people, as John says in the Apocalypse.

. . . And the chosen of the chosen are those who by reason of perfect knowledge are called [as the best] from the church itself and honored with the most august glory—the judges and rulers—twenty-four (the grace being doubled) equally from Jews and Greeks. For it is my opinion that the grades here in the church: bishops, presbyters, and deacons, are imitations of the angelic glory and of that economy which, the Scriptures say, awaits those who, following the footsteps of the apostles, have lived in perfection and righteousness according to the gospel. For they, when taken up in the clouds, as the apostle writes (1 Thess 4:17), will first minister, and then be classed in the presbyterate by promotion in glory (for glory differs from glory—1 Cor 15:41) till they grow into "a perfect man"—Eph 4:13. (Stromata VII 13)

The first paragraph states that the apostles were chosen precisely because, in the divine foreknowledge, they had been proven worthy. The second paragraph speaks of the Gnostic being a presbyter not by reason of ordination but by reason of virtue. Clement is aware of the tension between his idea of priesthood based on merit and the existence in the church of a priesthood based on ordination. His attempted answer, however, seems to be little more than a graceful evasion. Finally, in the third paragraph, Clement seems to prescind from the problem in order to present his picture of the ideal church.

Clement's ecclesiology—the above passage is typical—is quite vague, except for one point. He clearly sees the church as the guardian and guarantor of an orthodoxy which comes from the proper interpretation of Scripture in accordance with the apostolic traditions (see especially Stromata VII 16). Clement does not get very specific, but there is no reasonable doubt that, for him gnosis means ecclesiastical gnosis, and that the interpretation of Scripture is a church responsibility, however difficult it might be for us to determine what he might concretely have meant by this.

Gnostic martyrdom.[31] Like all early Christians, Clement sees in martyrdom the perfect work of love. But with the cool eye of reason he also rejects all reckless enthusiasm for it and any desire for it which stems from any motive but the love of God. He prefers, it seems, to emphasize the gnostic martyrdom of a life lived according to the Gospels:

> The Lord says in the Gospel, "Whoever shall leave father or mother or brethren," etc., "for the sake of the gospel and my name" (Matt 19:29), he is blessed; not indicating simple martyrdom, but the Gnostic martyrdom [cf. also Stromata IV 14], as of the man who has conducted himself according to the rule of the gospel, in love to the Lord. . . . (Stromata IV 4; cf. also IV 18)

Clement thus sees both blood martyrdom and Gnostic martyrdom as sacrificial, but without making much of the point. He prefers, it seems, the latter, but sees the virtue of love as towering over both.

5) *The Temple and the Altar.* Clement not only takes up the traditions which saw both the church and individual Christian as the true temple, and the soul(s) of the Christian(s) as the true altar;[32] he also develops this theme still further:

> . . . he who builds up the temple of God in men, that he may cause God to take up his abode in men. Cleanse the temple, and pleasures and amusements abandon to the winds and the fire, as a fading flower; but wisely cultivate the fruits of self-command, and present yourself to God as an offering of first fruits. (Protrepticus 11)

Here, for the first time in Christian literature, the idea of di-

31. Stromata IV 4 and 9–18 constitute a small tract on martyrdom.
32. Stromata II 20; IV 21; Paedagogus II 10: Quis dives salvetur 18:2.

vine indwelling is connected with the temple-cleansing which prepares both a worthy abode for God and a worthy place for offering Christian sacrifice. The Christian or true Gnostic is now not just the offering and the offerer but also the place of worship. In another work, Clement becomes the first Christian writer to think of the reception of the Eucharist as enshrining Christ within us as in a temple:

> Such is the suitable food which the Lord ministers, and he offers his flesh and pours forth his blood, and nothing is wanting for the children's growth. O amazing mystery! We are enjoined to cast off the old and carnal corruption, as also the old nutriment, receiving in exchange another new regimen, that of Christ, receiving him if we can, to hide him within and to enshrine the savior in our hearts so that we may correct the affections of our flesh. (Paedagogus I 6)

Clement can also speak of the heavenly temple (Stromata V 1), and of the whole church—in heaven as well as on earth—as temple (Stromata VI 14); but it was the temple here below, the temple of the Christian community and the individual Gnostic, which particularly captivated his attention. In developing this theme he brings the theology of Christian sacrifice to a new level of ecclesiological fullness far beyond what it had in any of the earlier Christian writings. We can illustrate this in a series of passages from Clement in which the center of attention shifts from spiritualizing temple criticism, to the church as temple, the Gnostic as temple, the community as altar, and finally to the individual soul as the altar from which rises the incense of holy prayer:

> How can he, to whom belongs everything that is, need anything? If God had a human form, he would, like man, have need of food, shelter, housing and what goes with these. Those who are similar in form and affections will require similar sustenance. And if the temple has two meanings, both God himself and the structure raised to his honor, is it not proper for us to apply the name of temple to the church which by holy knowledge came into being in God's honor? For it is of great value to God, not having been constructed by mechanical art nor embellished by an imposter's hand, but by the will of God fashioned into a temple. For it is not now the place but the assemblage

of the elect that I call the church. This temple is better for the reception of the greatness of the dignity of God. For the living creature, which is of high value, is made sacred by that which is worth all, or rather which has no equivalent in virtue of the exceeding sanctity of the latter. Now this is the Gnostic, who is of great value and who is honored by God. For in him God is enshrined, that is, the knowledge respecting God is consecrated. (Stromata VII 5)

The altar, then, that is with us here, the terrestrial one, is the congregation of those who devote themselves to prayers, having as it were one common voice and one mind. . . .

Now breathing together is properly said of the church. For the sacrifice of the church is the word breathing as incense from holy souls, the sacrifice and the whole mind being at the same time unveiled to God. . . . And will they not believe us when we say that the righteous soul is the truly sacred altar, and that incense arising from it is holy prayer? (Stromata VII 6)

There is much in the Scriptures and in Ignatius and Polycarp which might be seen as the background for this development. But a great deal of what we find here seems to be directly due to Clement's Christian interpretation of the Philonic tradition.

We can see, now, how much lies behind Clement's oft-repeated protestation (almost like a profession of faith) in which, speaking for the whole church, he affirms that the Gnostic worships God "not in a specified place, or selected temple [cf. Mal 1:11], or at certain festivals and on appointed days, but during his whole life in every place" (Stromata VII 7 and *passim*).

Origen: Christian Life as Sacrifice

Origen, more than any other, represents the Christian culmination of the spiritualizing development we have traced from its biblical origins. Thus, in consideration of Origen's preeminence as the great teacher of the ancient church, his massive influence on the great Fathers of the West as well as of the East, and the fact that he mentions sacrifice so frequently that Harnack calls him "the great theologian of sacrifice,"[33] even the brief sketch we

33. A. Harnack, *Lehrbuch der Dogmengeschichte* (3 vols.; 4th ed.; Tübingen: Mohr [Siebeck], 1909–10; repr. Darmstadt: Wissenschaftliche Buchgesellschaft, 1964), 1. 477. P. Nautin, *Origène. Sa vie et son oeuvre* (Paris: Beauchesne, 1977) is the best key to Origen studies.

can provide here might still be useful—especially since the material on which it is based has thus far appeared only in continental publications.[34] Still lacking is the full cultural, philosophical, and theological context which must necessarily qualify the analysis of a figure as complex and controversial as Origen. On the other hand, this sketch reveals the continuance in Origen of some major sacrificial themes, such as the idea of Christian life as sacrificial, which we have seen arise earlier in the Christian tradition.

As with Philo and Clement, the great Alexandrians before him, Origen's generally unsystematic method requires that a careful investigation of any particular theme be based on an analysis of all texts relevant to that theme. Complicating this task, but also making such a broadly based method all the more imperative, is the lack of reliability in the Latin translations of Rufinus and Jerome (early fifth century) in which the greater part of Origen's extant work has come down to us.[35]

Continuing the openness of Clement, his predecessor at Alexandria, Origen has a basically positive attitude toward Old Testament sacrifice which he repeatedly uses as the basis for spiritual or allegorical interpretations. Many of these interpretations move out into areas that have little to do with sacrifice. Our survey is thus based only on those passages in which, wherever he starts, Origen develops the meaning of sacrifice for Christians of his own day. The reader of this sketch will encounter a great deal of familiar territory. For Origen continually develops images and themes taken from the Jewish and Christian tradition which nourished him.

Although he did not write systematically, with the notable

34. R. J. Daly, "Sacrifice in Origen," *Studia Patristica XI* (TU 108; Berlin: Akademie-Verlag, 1972) 125–29; "Early Christian Influences on Origen's Concept of Sacrifice," *Origeniana*, ed. H. Crouzel, G. Lomiento, and J. Ruis-Camps; *Quaderni di Vetera Christianorum* 12 (1975) 312–26.

35. Of the roughly 550 passages in Origen which speak of sacrifice or related subjects, about 340 occur in the Latin translations, some 20 in the unreliable Greek fragments of the Commentary on the Psalms, and about 190 in well-attested Greek texts. Fortunately, these Greek texts alone are sufficient to demonstrate the major aspects of Origen's thought on sacrifice. The most important sources are, from the Greek: Commentary on Matthew, Exhortation to Martyrdom, Against Celsus, and, above all, the Commentary on John; and from the Latin: the homilies, particularly Rufinus' translation of the Homilies on Leviticus.

exception of the fairly early On First Principles, his thought was not without system. Familiarity with Origen enables us to see that despite the excesses of his allegorical imagination, there is a basic order underneath it all. This gives us some confidence that this sketch of Origen's thought on sacrifice is also truly representative of Christian theology at the outset of its first great flowering.

According to Origen, Jesus Christ is the central figure; he is the true Paschal Lamb who is led to the slaughter, who takes away the sins of the world, who by his own blood reconciles us to the Father. He emptied himself, bearing our infirmities and chastisements out of love for us and obedience to the Father. He is the great and perfect high priest, in fact both priest and victim in his perfect and unique offering to the Father. Yet in all this, it is the will of the Father and not primarily his own which Jesus carries out; the primary motivating agency is that of the Father's love.

But Origen's main concern seems to be to teach how the church and its members, and indeed the whole world, share in the sacrifice of Christ. For the true Jerusalem, he explains, is the church, built of living stones (cf. 1 Pet 2:5), where there is a holy priesthood and where spiritual sacrifices are offered to God by those who are spiritual (= Christian) and who have come to the knowledge of the law of the spirit.[36] As with most early Christian writers, martyrdom is the most perfect way to unite oneself to Christ and his sacrifice. The following sequence of ideas (from the Commentary on John VI 54) is typical of Origen: The bloodshedding of the martyrs is the sacrifice which is related to that of the Lamb. In the Book of Revelation, John sees the martyrs standing next to the heavenly altar of sacrifice. Then— after searching for the spiritual meaning of the sacrifice of Jephthah's daughter, which he finds in the vicarious nature of Christian sacrifice—Origen concludes that through the death of the pious martyrs many others receive blessings beyond description.

This "heavenly altar of sacrifice" introduces the eschatological

36. Cf. Origen, Commentary on John VI 59 (38) and XIII 13.

perspective and points up how Origen sees the meaning of sacrifices in the heavenly mysteries. For, drawing on the tradition of the metahistorical, triple dimensional aspects of the Passover (past-present-future; see above, pp. 39–40), Origen remarks that every festival which really belongs to the Lord awaits its consummation not here and now but in the coming age and in heaven when the kingdom comes. For worship in a place is only the pattern and shadow of the heavenly sacrifices. Our Passover, Christ, has been sacrificed (1 Cor 5:7), and will be sacrificed hereafter. We must, therefore, through the word, rise to the third Pasch that will be celebrated in the festive gathering of countless angels in a perfect and most holy Exodus (Commentary on John X 14 [11]–15[12]; 18 [13]).

Origen also develops the tradition, especially as it comes from Paul through Clement of Alexandria, which looks beyond martyrdom to see the whole of Christian life in terms of sacrifice.[37]

The rich development of the temple theme which we have traced from Paul, 1 Peter, Philo, Barnabas, and Clement of Alexandria, is also continued by Origen. He exhorts us to refuse to build merely lifeless temples; for our body is a temple of God, and the best of these temples is the body of Jesus Christ. ·The temple which has been destroyed will be rebuilt of living and most precious stones, with each of us becoming a precious stone in the great temple of God. As living stones we must also be active. For if, says Origen, I raise my hands in prayer, but leave hanging the hands of my soul instead of raising them with good and holy works, then the raising of my hands is not an evening sacrifice. In a concrete application, Origen remarks that good and holy speech is an offering to God, but bad speech is an offering to idols; and whoever listens to bad speech eats what has been offered to idols.[38]

True to the central Christian mystery of the incarnation, Origen also emphasizes the importance of the body in the sacrifice of the

37. Cf. Homilies on Leviticus 2, 4; Homilies on Joshua 2, 1; Commentary on the Psalms 49, 5.
38. Against Celsus VIII 19; Dialogue with Heraclides 20; Homilies on Numbers 20, 3.

Christian; for no one weak in soul and slow in words can offer the saving sacrifice. Thus, following the New Testament, Origen sees the gift worthy of God not in sacrifices or holocausts, but in the very life itself of the Christian. As he comments on the widow's offering, he reminds us that it is not what or how much we offer that is important, as long as it consists of all that we are and have, and as long as we offer it with our whole strength.[39]

Thus it is clear that all offering is vain unless we have the proper dispositions. The Lamb takes away the sins only of those who suffer. Thus, if we want to offer to God our proud flesh as a sacrificial calf, we must first mortify our members and live ascetically lest, after preaching to others, we fall away ourselves. Contact with Christ's sacrifice is saving, but only if one draws near to Jesus, the word made flesh, with full faith and obedience as did the woman with the hemorrhage who was healed by touching Christ's robe (Mark 5:25–34 parr). Origen never tries of stressing the need for the proper internal dispositions for sacrifice. For, following Clement of Alexandria's adaptation of Philo, as he sees it, the altar on which Christian sacrifice takes place is the altar within us.[40]

On this internal altar the Christian must offer without ceasing. Truly celebrating a feast means serving God faithfully, living ascetically and prayerfully, and continually offering to God bloodless sacrifices in prayer. For it is by constant prayer that we become living stones from which Jesus builds the altar on which to offer spiritual victims. Origen stresses the need for unceasing sacrifice by repeatedly referring to or expanding on Ps 44:22: "For thy sake we are slain all the day long, and accounted as sheep for the slaughter."[41]

39. Commentary on Romans IX (on Rom 12:1); Homilies on Leviticus 5, 12; Commentary on the Psalms 115; Homilies on Numbers 24, 2; Commentary on John XIX 7 (2) -8.

40. Homilies on Jeremiah 18, 10; Commentary on John VI 58 (37); Homilies on Leviticus 1, 5; 4, 8; Homilies on Numbers 24, 2; Commentary on the Lamentations of Jeremiah Fragment 49; Against Celsus VIII 17; Homilies on Leviticus 5, 3–4.

41. Commentary on John VI 52; Against Celsus VIII 21; Homilies on Joshua 9, 1; Commentary on the Psalms, PG 12, 1428A–B; Commentary on Romans VIII, PG 14, 1132; Exhortation to Martyrdom 21.

Before we move on to the Eucharist as sacrifice in the early church, we must take note of how Origen's idea of sacrifice has so little to do with liturgy or ritual. To look through Origen's work for the idea of Eucharist as sacrifice—let alone something more specific like "sacrifice of the Mass"—is to bypass his central thought and concentrate on something he obviously did not find relevant enough to command much of his attention. It is true that some of what Origen says makes sense only on the supposition that he conceived of the Christian liturgy as being in some way sacrificial. We must nevertheless keep in mind that when Origen thought of Christian sacrifice, that is, of what Christians do when they offer sacrifice, he thought as did the writers of the New Testament (see above, pp. 82–83): foremost in his mind was apparently not a liturgical rite of the church, but rather the internal liturgy of the Christian heart and spirit by which a person offers oneself and all one's prayers, works, and thoughts through Jesus Christ to God the Father.

THE EUCHARIST AS SACRIFICE

As mentioned in the Foreword, it is hoped that the following survey will provide a valuable boost to the process of Christian unity. My specific task, working from the background provided by this book, will be to try to present, in the context of the primitive church, and on its terms, not ours, just what was for the early church the inner dynamic of the Eucharist.[42]

The accounts of eucharistic institution in the New Testament provide the obvious starting point (1 Cor 11:23–26; Mark 14:22–25; Matt 26:26–29; Luke 22:14–20). These accounts, within the liturgy of the primitive church, re-present the Lord's Supper (see above, pp. 56–58). They indicate that the primitive church saw the eucharistic celebration either as a sacrificial event or, at least, as an event laden with sacrificial connotations. However, from our vantage points in the churches today, it is not easy to distinguish between the sacrificial overtones which may have been

---

42. See CS, 498–508. Extensive detail is provided by H. Moll, *Die Lehre von der Eucharistie als Opfer. Eine dogmengeschichtliche Untersuchung von Neuen Testament bis Irenaeus von Lyon* (Theophaneia 26; Cologne/Bonn: Hanstein, 1975).

actually intended by the New Testament writers, and the much broader sacrificial overtones which we, after the fact, might perceive to be present or latent in the New Testament.

Early rabbinic Judaism, and hence also the primitive Christianity which took its roots from it, saw the Passover as a sacrificial rite (see above, pp. 38–41). Hence the care taken by the evangelists to situate the Last Supper in the framework of the Passover celebration adds an obvious sacrificial dimension to it, all the more so since the connection among Christ, Passover, and sacrifice was apparently already established in the tradition (cf. 1 Cor 5:7: "Christ our Passover Lamb has been sacrificed").

The evangelists also seem to present the Last Supper as a prophecy-in-act anticipation of Christ's sacrificial death. This is similar—although here in a Christian sacramental sense—to Ezekiel acting out his prophecy of the impending destruction of Jerusalem (Ezek 4 and 5). The prophetic action signified that the prophesied event had already become real, even though its concrete historical (and now absolutely inevitable) unfolding still remained in the future. For the Christian Eucharist this at least implies a sacrificial dimension, since the early church in its liturgy was consciously re-presenting the Last Supper, that is, it was consciously doing what the Lord Jesus did the night before he died.

The words over the cup mentioning the blood of the (new) covenant powerfully evoke the unique Exodus covenant sacrifice (Exod 24:3–8; see above, pp. 37–38). They doubtlessly helped the early Christians to see, specifically in the Eucharist, and not just generally in the Christ-event, the fulfillment of Old Testament sacrifice. Similarly, the synoptic words "shed for many (you)" could not but have reminded the first Christians of the blood rites which were of vital importance in all Old Testament animal sacrifice.[43] Matthew's addition, "for the forgiveness of sin," points this recollection toward the atoning, sin-forgiving function of sacrifice and, more specifically, of the sin offering itself.

43. E.g., the Epistle to the Hebrews actually repeats the rabbinic dictum: "Without the shedding of blood there is no forgiveness of sin" (Heb 9:22).

Servant-of-God Christology, and in particular the violent death of the Suffering Servant, is evoked by the mention of "blood being shed" and the various "for you" and "for many" phrases modifying the eucharistic body and blood. For "body" and "blood" do not seem to refer primarily to the sacrificial elements of flesh and blood, but rather to the martyrological idea inherent in Servant Christology.[44] The sacrificial overtones here are quite strong, although we cannot be sure how consciously present they were to those involved in the primitive levels of New Testament formation. In the context of the gospel emphasis on Jesus' personal self-giving, the phrase "my body *given for you*" also evokes sacrificial overtones. For this theme is the very heart of the theology of the Akedah (sacrifice of Isaac) which represented the Jewish sacrificial soteriology familiar to the primitive Palestinian Christian communities (see above, pp. 47–52).

The commemorative eucharistic command, "Do this in memory of me," also roots the New Testament Lord's Supper more solidly in a sacrificial context. For this command cannot be explained adequately without reference to the *anamnesis* motif of the Passover feast, and possibly also of the Akedah. Finally 1 Corinthians 10 hangs together only on the supposition that Paul and his Corinthians looked upon the Eucharist as a sacrifice of the communion type.

The cumulative effect of this evidence is quite cogent. It necessarily inclines us to conclude that the New Testament church considered the Lord's Supper and its own liturgical representation of it to be, at least in the broad sense of the word, a sacrificial event. For it is unlikely in the extreme that the New Testament writers could have been totally unaware of the sacrificial connotations of their own words. In terms of later development, these sacrificial connotations are more than adequate to explain how writers such as Justin, Irenaeus, and Hippolytus

---

44. I follow here the basic position of J. Betz, *Die Eucharistie in der Zeit der Griechischen Väter* I/1 (Freiburg: Herder, 1955) 41, 46–50; II/1 (2d ed., 1964) 21, 38–41, 131 over against that of J. Jeremias, *The Eucharistic Words of Jesus* (trans. N. Perrin; New York: Scribner's, 1966; reprinted Philadelphia: Fortress, 1977) 198–201; 221–22. Cf. *CS*, 222–25.

could think of themselves as faithfully interpreting the Scriptures when they spoke of the Eucharist as sacrifice.

The Didache (see above, pp. 84–85), the earliest of the church orders (late first or early second century A.D.), may also be the earliest nonbiblical Christian writing to mention the Eucharist, chapters 9 and 10 being primitive eucharistic prayers. They contain nothing specifically sacrificial but in their present form they had already undergone some development and were apparently no longer in use as the central eucharistic prayer of the liturgy. In Didache 14, however, sacrifice is explicitly central. The breaking of the bread and offering of thanks "on the Lord's own day," as well as the requirement to confess one's sins "so that your sacrifice may be pure" (14:1), clearly designate the event being prepared for as a sacrificial eucharistic liturgy, while 14:2 adds the admonition: "Lest your sacrifice be defiled," and 14:3 concludes by rephrasing Mal 1:11 from a prophecy to a command to offer pure sacrifice to the name of the Lord. Thus, the idea of the Eucharist as sacrifice is taken for granted. However, there is no account of the content of this Eucharist or eucharistic prayer, nor is there any explanation of the Didache's understanding of the term sacrifice.

Clement of Rome's First Letter to the Corinthians (see above, pp. 85–86) uses sacrificial terms and concepts to describe the public life and liturgy of the church. *1 Clem* 44:3–4 clearly understands the bishop to have a special and specifically sacrificial function in the church's worship. But when 44:4 speaks of this function as "offering the sacrifices" (i.e., gifts), Clement seems to be using "sacrifice" in the highly spiritualized Christian sense of the prayer of praise and thanksgiving. For it does not seem possible, as it is later on with Justin (*1 Apol.* 65:3; 66:2), to interpret the gifts which are offered and for which one gives thanks as referring primarily to the Eucharist, i.e., the bread and wine which are the flesh and blood of the incarnate Jesus. This would be to project back into Clement's words the understanding of later writers.

Ignatius of Antioch does not, in the more precise sense of these terms, write of the Eucharist as sacrifice. But if by "Eucharist" we understand the church's public prayer of praise and thanks-giving, and if we understand "sacrifice" in the spiritualized sense unfolded in this study, we can indeed speak of the Eucharist as sacrifice in Ignatius. Several texts speak of the church or gathered community as an altar or place of sacrifice (Ign. *Eph.* 5:2; Ign. *Trall.* 7:2; Ign. *Phld.* 4; Ign. *Magn.* 7:2). A few other passages suggest that Ignatius, if not already explicitly aware of it, would have at least warmly welcomed the idea of the Eucharist of Christ's body and blood as sacrificial. Ign. *Smyrn.* 7:1 evokes the sacrificial overtones of the Servant-of-God Christology by speaking of "the flesh of our Savior . . . which suffered for our sins." In Ign. *Rom.* 2:2 Ignatius looks ahead to his martyrdom in terms which are both sacrificial ("that I be sacrified to God while the altar is still prepared") and liturgical (the community gathered around the altar singing "praise to the Father through Christ Jesus"). The sacrificial-eucharistic idea is also strengthened where Ignatius speaks of being the wheat of God and of becoming the pure bread of Christ, "that by these things I may be found a sacrifice (Ign. *Rom.* 4:1-2).

For *Justin Martyr*, however, it seems clear that *Christian sacrifice is the Eucharist* (see above, pp. 87-90). It is not quite so easy, however, to state precisely what Justin might mean by this.

Justin fiercely rejects pagan and Jewish sacrifice and emphatically insists that Christians also offer sacrifice—when they celebrate the Eucharist of the bread and the cup. This alone is the fulfillment of Mal 1:10-12 (*Dial.* 29:1; 41; 116; 117). Whether or not Justin intended to identify the Eucharist with Christian sacrifice, the fact is that whenever he becomes specific about the sacrifices which Christians offer, he is always talking about the Eucharist or, more precisely, the eucharistic prayer. This suggests that the inner dynamic of the eucharistic prayer holds the key to Justin's idea of Christian sacrifice.

In the Eucharist, the divine Logos forms flesh and blood for himself just as he did in the incarnation (cf. esp. *1 Apol.* 33; 46:5; 66). The prayer of the leader of the Eucharist is thus seen as a "memorial" of the incarnation, as invoking the saving presence of the Logos via the hallowing or "eucharistizing" of the elements of bread and wine now made into the flesh and blood of the Lord by the power of the Logos. For Justin, therefore, Christian sacrifice (sacrifices which Christians offer) seems to be first and foremost the prayer of praise and thanksgiving pronounced "over" or "before" or "on the occasion of the offering of" the bread and the cup. Justin was apparently the first to call this food in this sense *Eucharist*.

Irenaeus of Lyons (see above, pp. 91–98) also uses "Eucharist" to refer to the body and blood of the Lord (*Adv. Haer.* IV 31:4). But he also goes further in speaking of the eucharistic bread and cup as "the new oblation of the new covenant" (*Adv. Haer.* IV 29:5). In somewhat more detail than Justin, Irenaeus seems to associate the essence of the eucharistic sacrifice with prayer. *Adv. Haer.* IV 30:1, while speaking of Mal 1:10–12, refers to Rev. 8:4 in order to show that the incense of the Malachi prophecy is "the prayers of the saints." *Adv. Haer* IV 31:1–3 takes this "offering of the church" which has already been shown to be the Eucharist, and explains it further so that it not only means prayers but also includes in some way the good dispositions, works, and lives of the Christians. Thus, in the context of the early Christian spiritualization of sacrifice, we can conclude that for Irenaeus, as for Justin, the Eucharist was a sacrifice not in its cultic action, but more precisely in its prayers and thanksgivings.

For *Hippolytus* (see above, pp. 98–100), the idea of the Eucharist as sacrifice is central, for the Apostolic Tradition presents the Eucharist as a highly institutionalized sacrificial rite. "Oblation" (*prosphora*) signifies both the eucharistic rite as a whole and the material itself of the offering. In the *memores* and *epiclesis* of the eucharistic anaphora we read:

> Mindful therefore of his death and resurrection, we offer you the bread and the chalice, giving thanks to you for having counted us worthy to stand before you and serve you. And we ask that you send your Holy Spirit upon the offering of the holy church. (Apostolic Tradition 4)

These words, reminiscent of Irenaeus' "new oblation of the new testament," obviously take for granted the idea of the Eucharist as sacrifice. They also show the church both offering with thanksgiving and receiving the bread and the cup which are identified with the physically incarnate body and blood of Christ. For the whole rite is understood as recalling or re-presenting before God the redemptive work of Christ and as making him present and operative for the community.

The actual center of Hippolytus' idea of the Eucharist as sacrifice is found in the way he develops further the Logos-theology of the eucharistic memorial (begun by Irenaeus; see above, pp. 93–94): Against Noetus 4 (see above, p. 98) explains that it is by the *Pneuma* (i.e., Spirit, or divine mode of being of the Logos) that the Logos brings about both his historical and eucharistic incarnations. Hence Hippolytus' close association of incarnation with eucharistic sacrifice, and the suggestion in Against Noetus 4 that the purpose of the incarnation was for the divine Logos to offer to the Father in heaven his incarnate flesh (= his eucharistic body and blood). This is what is "memorialized" in the eucharistic anaphora.

In its inner dynamic, however, the action of this sacrificial event is performed ultimately only by the divine spirit or Logos. In what way, then, did Hippolytus understand Christians themselves to offer sacrifice? As a result of this study we can say, as Hippolytus himself seems to, that the *prayer* of the bishop as he gives thanks over the bread and the cup (with the words of institution apparently understood as the *object* of the thanksgiving) is a sacrificial act. For Hippolytus this seems to be the central sacrificial act of the church.

Thus, from the point of view of that which is liturgical or sacramental, the idea of the Eucharist as sacrifice reaches an unmistakable high point in Hippolytus. But from another vitally important point of view, there has been a concomitant shift in emphasis which many historians and theologians could not characterize as a positive development. For the idea of Christian sacrifice (i.e., sacrifices which Christians offer) had begun to shift away from the practical living of the Christian life toward the church's public liturgical celebration of the Eucharist. The dominant New Testament idea, that the life and activity of

Christian people are themselves the sacrifice which they offer, does not seem even to be mentioned in Hippolytus. It seems to be wholly replaced by the idea of the Eucharist as sacrifice, in which the central sacrificial act is the divine Logos offering his incarnate (and eucharistic) body and blood to the Father. Secondarily, but also apparently increasingly dominant in the consciousness of those participating in the Eucharist, is the idea that the presiding bishop or priest offers—and that he alone is qualified to offer—the Eucharist. This consisted in offering the eucharistic prayer of praise and thanksgiving, that is, offering the gifts of bread and wine which are the flesh and blood of the Lord.

Seminally present, therefore, are two later—and, from the time of the Reformation, highly controversial—developments in eucharistic theology: 1) the idea that the Eucharist is a sacrifice which can be "offered" only by a minister or priest specially ordained for this purpose, and 2) the idea that this sacrifice offered by the priest is a fully real, cultic sacrifice.

CONCLUSION

We first recall the claim we made in the Foreword and at the end of Chapter One: that a proper understanding of the concept of Christian sacrifice is basic to a proper understanding of Christianity itself. It is anything but a matter of indifference to us that we find the early Christians from the New Testament onward understanding the Christ-event as a sacrificial event, looking upon the Eucharist, the central act of Christian worship, as a sacrifice, and speaking of the practical living of the Christian life as sacrificial. For we, no less than the first Christians, see the Christ-event as the origin, center, and goal of our own existence. We too celebrate the Eucharist as our central act of worship, and understand the way we live to be the best test of the authenticity of our Christianity.

One might well protest that sacrificial terms and concepts have, at most, only symbolic value for a technological age. One might suggest that we would be well advised to forget about sacrifice and to concentrate instead on the religious reality underlying these terms and concepts. For we do not offer animals in sacrifice; still less do we believe that the forgiveness of sins is tied up with certain sacrificial blood rites. But then, *neither did the early Christians*. They were, in fact, reproached as irreligious by their pagan neighbors because they neither offered sacrifice nor worshiped in temples. But, despite their radical rejection of both pagan and Jewish sacrifice, the first Christians continued to speak not only of the sacrifice of Christ, but also of themselves as the new temple, and of their own lives as sacrificial.

The sweep of our study has uncovered two distinct trends in

135

the origin and development of the Christian concept of sacrifice. There is a primary, spiritualizing trend, within which we can distinguish three significant phases; and, at least partially in tension with this, there is a secondary, institutionalizing trend.

The first phase of the spiritualizing trend has its roots deep in the Old Testament; for it is already well underway when, even as early as the tenth century Yahwistic accounts of Noah's sacrifice (Gen 8) and of the sacrifices of Cain and Abel (Gen 4), the sacred writers insist with increasing explicitness on the vital importance of the religious dispositions with which one offers sacrifice. This spiritualizing trend is also apparent in the theology of the divine acceptance of sacrifice (see above, pp. 21–25), especially in the insistence that it is God and not man who decides what is acceptable. And what God decides is acceptable does not remain wholly concealed in the inscrutability of the divine will. It is progressively revealed in the covenant theology of the prophets and Deuteronomist. In these writings it is quite clear that sacrifices offered by those failing to live up to the covenantal demands of justice and mercy are considered to be simply "not pleasing" or "not acceptable" or even "hateful" in the eyes of God. But material sacrifice is not thereby done away with, for this prophetic criticism makes sense only under the presupposition of the continued validity of the sacrificial system. What is achieved here is not precisely a rejection of the sacrificial cult, but rather the all-important realization that without the proper religious and ethical dispositions, material sacrifice (and, by implications, all external religious observance) is worthless.

With the completion of the first phase of the spiritualizing trend, even though proper dispositions are now seen as absolutely essential, the effective or dynamic center of sacrifice still seems to be the actual performance of the sacrificial ceremony. But as we move into the second phase of the spiritualizing trend, largely a post-exilic development, this center clearly shifts from the ceremony to the dispositions themselves.

An apparently strong catalyst for this change was the experience of exile and diaspora. Increasing numbers of Jews who continued to believe in the necessity of material sacrifice were prevented by geography from actively participating in sacrifice at the Jerusalem temple, the one place where sacrifice could validly be offered. Increasingly, the notion took root that what brought about reconciliation, atonement, and communion with God was not the actual performance of the sacrifices, but the fact that one performed them *according to the law*, that is, in accordance with the will of God.

This shift helped make it possible for the Qumran sectarians, while separated from the temple, to develop a theology of sacrificial atonement which looked upon their own community as the new temple, and the pious works performed by the community as taking the place of the atoning sacrifices materially offered in the Jerusalem temple. It also helped make it possible for Judaism to survive the loss of the temple after A.D. 70. For once the value of sacrifice was seen precisely as an act of obedient piety, it was not difficult to see other acts of obedient piety as being able to accomplish what was previously thought to be achievable only by ritual sacrifice.

It is in this context that Philo, writing in diaspora Alexandria, so emphasizes the internal religious dispositions for sacrifice that the external action or ceremony is accorded only symbolic significance. Much of the extremity of Philo's position is due to the antimaterial bias of his basically Platonistic philosophy. Christian thought, on the other hand, which draws a great deal from Philo, is generally preserved from the extremes of a radically antimaterial spiritualization by its own antidualistic faith both in God's creation of the material world and in the historical, bodily incarnation of the Logos. Christian sacrifice, therefore, both in its perfect realization in Jesus Christ, and in its imperfect realizations in his followers, is both spiritual *and* bodily.

However, this "bodiliness" of Christian sacrifice is far from being a mere nonspiritualized remnant of Old Testament sacrifice which has somehow survived the process of spiritualization. Even the bodiliness of Christian sacrifice grows, in its own way, out of this process. For the spiritualization process is not complete merely in the first phase when the internal dispositions are seen as absolutely essential; nor is spiritualization complete even in the second phase when the real center of sacrifice as a religious act has shifted completely to the dispositions and away from the external ceremony which is now viewed as wholly secondary, merely symbolic, or, as in Philo, even superfluous. Something vitally essential for incarnational Christianity is still missing.

The spiritualizing trend reaches its culmination in a specifically incarnational spiritualization. We claim, as the proven thesis of this work, that it is precisely an *incarnational spiritualization of sacrifice* that is operative in the New Testament and the early church. This incarnational spiritualization moves beyond the initial phase where dispositions are emphasized while ceremonial action remains central, and it moves beyond the second phase where ceremonial action becomes almost superfluous, to a third phase where, to the vital importance of proper dispositions, is now added the importance of incarnating proper dispositions in human action. The insights of phases one and two are taken up into a new incarnationally spiritualized notion of sacrifice described in terms of the performance of down-to-earth, practical, diaconal, ministerial, and apostolic works of the Christian life.

Theologically, or systematically, our work has now reached a certain natural climax. For the third phase of the spiritualization process yields a basic concept of sacrifice which is as applicable to the sacrifices of Christians as it is to the sacrifice of Christ. For Jesus, the dispositions are those of obedience and love to the Father *to whom* he offers, and those of self-sacrificing love and service to and for us *for whom* he offers. Christans are called to embody these same dispositions of obedience and love toward God, and of self-sacrificing love and service to and for the brothers and sisters. In Jesus, these dispositions do not remain internal; they are fleshed out or incarnated in his ministerial deeds of preaching, healing, teaching, and forgiving which culminate in the total and victorious self-giving of his Passion and resurrection. So too in the true follower of Jesus the internal dispositions for spiritualized sacrifice are not needed just for prayer and worship; they must above all be incarnated in the practical, diaconal, and ministerial deeds of the Christian life. Otherwise the Christian spiritualizing (or "christologizing") of sacrifice is not complete.

However, although our concept of Christian sacrifice seems to be basically complete, the story or history of Christian sacrifice is not. As we indicated above, there is in the history of Christian sacrifice, and somewhat in tension with the spiritualizing trend, a secondary, institutionalizing trend. An understanding of this trend affords valuable insights into a number of important contemporary theological and ecumenical issues, especially regarding the Eucharist. For it is indeed in the early development of the Christian Eucharist that this institutionalizing trend is located.

As we pointed out above, the New Testament accounts of institution indicate that the primitive church saw the Eucharist as sacrificial. Further, as we traced the development of eucharistic theology through the first two Christian centuries and searched the early eucharistic texts to find precisely what concept of sacrifice might have been operative in them, several points emerged with varying degrees of clarity.

First, most of what we have just described as the first two phases of the spiritualization process seems to be assumed without question and without exception. That is, the internal religious/ethical dispositions with which one offers sacrifice or takes part in sacrificial worship are seen to be the absolutely essential center of the religious acts which are spoken of or thought of as sacrificial. The evidence for this is overwhelming, and against it there appears to be no contradiction.

Second, what we described as the third phase of the spiritualization process, that is, the replacement of an actual offering of material sacrifice with following Christ in the practical, diaconal, or devotional works of Christian life and ministry, seems also to be supported by considerable evidence. For when we examined Justin, Irenaeus, and Hippolytus (the first Christian writers to begin to develop a eucharistic theology) to find out precisely what their concept of the "sacrificial action" in the celebration of the Eucharist was, we found that the sacrificial action did not appear to be, at least not primarily, the actual performance of the ceremony or the ritual action of the bishop or president of the assembly. It seemed to be primarily the *prayer* of the bishop—that is, one of those actions which in the spiritualization of sacrifice had come to be seen as replacing material sacrifice. One cannot claim absolute certitude for this conclusion but, in the context of the early Christian idea of sacrifice uncovered in this study, no other conclusion seems viable.

Finally, in Justin, Irenaeus, and especially Hippolytus, one can detect growing evidence of an institutionalizing trend which not only tends to institutionalize Christian eucharistic worship, but also begins to reintroduce what seems to have been superseded in the third phase of the institutionalizing trend: the idea that the performance of the ritual action is a sacrifice. Strongly sacramental traditions such as Roman Catholicism resonate vibrantly with this and tend to find in such texts early evidence for their theology of the sacrifice of the Mass.

The full history of this institutionalizing trend has not yet been written, at least not yet in a way that seems wholly satisfactory to scholars from the different Christian communions, although the ecumenical tone of our age suggests that this goal may now be within reach. However, full agreement among the churches on the theological significance of this history seems to lie much, much farther down the road. All the more reason, then, for us to underline in conclusion the unequivocally clear results of this study:

For the New Testament church, Christian sacrifice was not a cultic but rather an ethical idea, an idea that could include prayer and worship in the formal sense, but was not constituted by them. It was centered not in a formal act of cultic or external ceremonial worship but rather in the everyday practical life of Christian virtue, in the apostolic and charitable work of being a good Christian, of being "for others" as Christ was "for us." It was a totally free and loving response, carried out on the practical level of human existence, to Christ's act of self-giving love.

That is what Christian sacrifice was for the writers of the New Testament, and, to the extent that we are truly Christian, that is what it must also be for us today. Thus, no matter how similarly or differently we might understand the institutional or ecclesiological ramifications of celebrating the Eucharist, unless we do so with the fully spiritualized (= christologized) dispositions of Christian sacrifice, we call upon ourselves the stern rebuke Paul leveled against the Corinthians: "It is not the Lord's Supper which you celebrate" (1 Cor 11:20).

INDEXES

GENERAL

NOTE: A broad principle of selection was followed in compiling this index. Themes and their interconnections have been indexed even when the evidence for them was weak. Thus, the presence of some subjects here does not necessarily imply substantial evidence in their favor. Particularly important references are printed in **boldface**.

141

REFERENCES

OLD TESTAMENT

Genesis
1—11 — 11
2—3 — 12
4 — 136
4:3–7 — 5
4:4–7 — **23**
8 — 12, **15**, 136
8:20 — 14, 105
8:20–21 — **15**
8:20ff — 5
8:20—9:17 — 37
8:21 — 6, 21
9:4 — 25, 31, 32
15 — 12, 19, 37
18:22–23 — 33
22 — 8, **47–52**
22:1–14 — 14, **15**
22:2 — 41, 50, 51
33:9–11 — **21**
34 — 41
49:10–12 — 92
49:11 — 88

Exodus
3:1–6 — 19
4:24–26 — **41–43**
4:25 — 42
4:26 — 42
10:25 — 14
12 — 31, 33, 39, 101
12:13 — 42
12:22 — 41, 78
12:42 — 48
12:43–45 — 42
12:46 — 78

12:48 — 42
13:8 — 39
16:7–10 — 19
19:6 — 66, 67
19:16–24 — 19
20:24 — 14
20:25 — 110
24:3–8 — 31, **37–38**, 56, **128**
24:5 — 14
24:15–18 — 19
30:34–36 — 114
32:4–6 — 59
32:6 — 14, 16
32:30–32 — 33
40:34–38 — 19

Leviticus
1—2 — 13
1—7 — 38
1:2–12 — 16
1:5 — 38
1:6 — 113
1:7 — 17
1:11 — 38
3 — 13, 38
3:2 — 38
3:8 — 38
3:13 — 38
4 — 13, 16, 31
4:5–7 — 38
5 — 13, 16
6 — 18
6:8–9 — 17
6:12–13 — 17
6:26–30 — 13

7:6–10 — 13
7:14 — 38
10:1–2 — 17, 20
10:2 — 19
10:6 — 27
10:16–20 — 13
12 — 16
16 — 16, 17, 28, 31, 38, 88
16:13 — 19, 20
16:21 — 29
16:21–22 — **29**
16:23–24 — 115
17:11 — 25, **31–35**
17:14 — 25, 31, 32
22:27 — 49

Numbers
1:53 — 27
3:4 — 17, 20
4:1–16 — 17
9:12 — 78
15:1–10 — 16
16:35 — 19
16:46–50 — 20
17:11 — 27
18:5 — 27
19 — 38, 111
26:21 — 17, 20
28:1—29:40 — 16
28:6 — 16

Deuteronomy
16 — 39
16:1–6 — 39

Joshua
5:2–9 — 42

Judges
6:19–24 — 19
6:25–32 — 16
11:29–40 — 16
13:15–20 — 19

1 Samuel
6:14 — 16
14:45 — 33
26:19 — **22**

2 Samuel
12:13 — 28
24:17 — 33

1 Kings
5 — 17
8:10–11 — 19
18:17–40 — 16
18:20–38 — 15
18:30–40 — 19

2 Kings
16:15 — 16

2 Chronicles
5:14 — 19
7:1–3 — **18**
7:2 — 19
29:31–35 — 16
30:21–27 — 40
35:1–19 — 40

Ezra
3:1–6 —16

Psalms
34:20 — 78
44:22 — 126

MODERN AUTHORS